IT'S OBVIOUS YOU WON'T SURVIVE BY YOUR WITS ALONE

IT'S OBVIOUS YOU WON'T SURVIVE BY YOUR WITS ALONE

BRAINS

Competitors
Beavers
You

A DILBERT BOOK
BY SCOTT ADAMS

Andrews and McMeel
A Universal Press Syndicate Company
Kansas City

Introduction

I created the first five Dilbert books strictly to earn money. This sixth book is being done for love. Specifically, my love of money.

I don't mean I "love" money in some greedy, shallow sense of the word. I mean I actually have feelings for money. I once had a fling with an attractive little five dollar bill. It was wonderful, if you don't count the paper cuts . . . and of course there was the big fight after my tasteless joke about Ford's Theater. But mostly it was good.

It ended like most of my relationships — I traded her for a bag of Ruffles and a Diet Coke. The moral of the story is, "Don't fall in love on an empty stomach," especially if your loved one is accepted as legal tender at convenience stores.

Speaking of hunger, at parties I'm often asked if I see myself more as a writer or an artist. To which I reply, "Excuse me while I freshen my Snapple*." Then I scurry away. I escape because the conversation inevitably degenerates into unpleasant comparisons of my artwork and things found in nature, such as carpet stains and motorcycle accidents.

I'm sure my artwork would be better if I spent more time on it, but I'm a busy guy. Take today for instance; I have to write an exciting introduction for this book. Later I'll be sorting all of my currency into "cute" and "ugly" piles. This stuff doesn't happen by itself.

Here's my point: Wouldn't it be nice if all the annoying people on earth became our personal servants? Well, it's possible. As you may already know, when Dogbert conquers the planet and becomes supreme ruler, anybody who is not on the free Dilbert newsletter mailing list will become domestic servants for the enlightened people who are. Save yourself from that fate by joining now.

The Dilbert newsletter is free and it's published approximately "whenever I feel like it," which is about four times a year.

E-mail subscription (preferred): write to scottadams@aol.com

Snail mail: Dilbert Mailing List c/o United Media
                 200 Madison Ave.
                 New York, NY 10016

Scott Adams

http://www.unitedmedia.com/comics/dilbert/

* It's not what you think. You're disgusting.

DILBERT By Scott Adams

DILBERT, I'D LIKE YOU TO INTRODUCE THE NEW GUY TO EVERYBODY.

GROAN

THIS WAY I NEVER HAVE TO LEARN THEIR NAMES.

THE FIRST STOP ON OUR ODYSSEY IS BUD.

UH... BUD, THIS IS THE NEW GUY, AND VICE-VERSA.

WHAT'S THIS?! ANOTHER PINK-BOTTOMED, IVY LEAGUE, MANAGEMENT "TRAINEE"?!

NEWS

IN MY DAY, YOU HAD TO START AT THE BOTTOM... AND BY GOLLY, YOU STAYED THERE!!

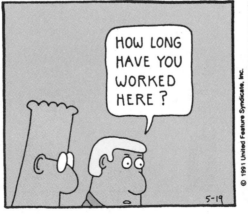

HOW LONG HAVE YOU WORKED HERE?

5-19

A WEEK... THIS HAPPENS PRETTY QUICKLY.

10

DILBERT
By Scott Adams

WELCOME TO DOGBERT'S "SCHOOL OF HARD KNOCKS."

THIS IS THE SCHOOL YOU'VE HEARD SO MUCH ABOUT.

CHANCES ARE, ONE OF YOUR PARENTS IS A GRADUATE OF THIS SCHOOL.

© 1991 United Feature Syndicate, Inc.

AT DOGBERT'S SCHOOL OF HARD KNOCKS, YOU WILL GAIN THE WISDOM THAT CAN ONLY BE OBTAINED THROUGH SUFFERING.

THROUGHOUT THE COURSE, I'LL BE WHACKING YOU WITH VARIOUS BLUNT OBJECTS.

IT MAY BE UNPLEASANT AT FIRST, BUT YOU'LL GET USED TO IT.

EVENTUALLY, YOUR BRAIN WILL RATIONALIZE THE WHOLE EXPERIENCE. YOU'LL THINK I'M A DEDICATED TEACHER, AND YOU'LL ACTUALLY BELIEVE YOU LEARNED SOMETHING.

STICK WITH THE BASICS, I SAY.

5-26

THE DIFFERENCE
BETWEEN
MEN AND WOMEN

(WELL, ONE OF THEM)

DILBERT

By Scott Adams

What are you working on?

I'm writing my own encyclopedia to sell for large profits.

How could you write an entire encyclopedia by yourself?

It's abridged. I had to cut some corners to get it all in five pages.

© 1991 United Feature Syndicate, Inc.

Five pages?! You condensed the history and knowledge of the world into five pages?!!

Actually, it's mostly about me ... the other stuff didn't seem important.

6-9

But I threw in some stuff about Canada to make it seem thorough.

"Canada has trees."

I'll have to tighten that section a bit.

S. Adams

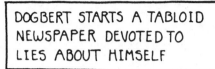

DOGBERT STARTS A TABLOID NEWSPAPER DEVOTED TO LIES ABOUT HIMSELF

WHERE DO YOU GET YOUR IDEAS?

"DOGBERT'S IMPATIENCE WITH FOOLS WAS LEGENDARY. HE ONCE CHOKED A MAN BY HIS NECKTIE FOR ASKING STUPID QUESTIONS."

"IT HAPPENED ONE DAY WHEN THE FOOL WAS READING OVER DOGBERT'S SHOULDER AND GOT TOO CLOSE."

IT'S GOING TO BE ANOTHER YEAR OF FLOGGING DEAD HORSES.

BUT SOMEHOW WE'LL MUDDLE THROUGH OUR INTERNAL BUREAUCRACY, GOUGE OUR CUSTOMERS, AND KEEP GETTING OUR TINY PAYCHECKS.

SIR, WILSON TURNED INTO A CLUMP OF UNINSPIRED SOD.

IT'S JUST AS WELL; HE HAD A BAD ATTITUDE.

YOU KNOW THAT GOOD FEELING YOU GET WHEN YOU FIRST PUT A Q-TIP IN YOUR EAR?

YEAH.

CAN I FREELY ENJOY IT, OR IS IT A SIN?

I THINK IT'S OKAY.

GOOD, BECAUSE I USED A WHOLE BOX YESTERDAY.

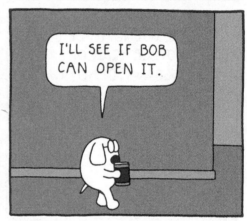

YOU'VE BEEN RANDOMLY SELECTED TO HAVE LUNCH WITH A SENIOR EXECUTIVE OF THE COMPANY.

THIS IS HOW THE EXECUTIVES SHOW THAT THEY ARE REGULAR PEOPLE, JUST LIKE YOU AND ME.

AT LUNCH

I COULD SQUASH YOU LIKE A BUG! HA HA HA HA HA HA!

DILBERT IS CHOSEN TO HAVE LUNCH WITH AN EXECUTIVE.

I WANT YOU TO KNOW THAT I'M JUST A NORMAL GUY...

OH, SURE, I MAKE A LITTLE MORE MONEY, AND I HAVE A NICE OFFICE...

AND OF COURSE, I'M MUCH, MUCH SMARTER.

LUNCH WITH A TOP EXECUTIVE

I HAVE THESE LUNCHES TO FIND OUT WHAT THE WORKERS ARE THINKING. YOU MAY SPEAK FREELY.

OKAY... IT SEEMS LIKE THE COMPANY IS LACKING LEADERSHIP AND DIRECTION. THE EXECUTIVES SQUELCH ALL INITIATIVE BY PUNISHING THOSE WHO TAKE RISKS AND VOICE OPINIONS.

YOU LEAVE ME LITTLE CHOICE BUT TO FLING THIS AU GRATIN POTATO AT YOUR FOREHEAD.

HOW WAS YOUR LUNCH WITH THE EXECUTIVE VICE PRESIDENT?

EVERYTHING WAS FINE UNTIL THE FOOD FIGHT. HE STARTED THROWING AU GRATIN POTATOES... I COUNTERED WITH AN EAR OF CORN TO HIS HEAD AND RAN FOR THE EXIT.

WHEN I LEFT, HE WAS FACE-DOWN IN THE CLAM CHOWDER AND THE KITCHEN STAFF WAS SINGING "DING-DONG THE WITCH IS DEAD."

YOU'RE UNDER ARREST FOR KILLING A SENIOR EXECUTIVE OF YOUR COMPANY WITH AN EAR OF CORN.

IT...IT WAS SELF-DEFENSE! HE STARTED THE FOOD FIGHT! I HAD JUST SEASONED MY CORN... IT WAS IN MY HAND... IT WAS JUST A REFLEX!!

THE CHARGE IS "A SALT AND BUTTERING WITH INTENT TO KILL"

WHAT ARE YOU IN FOR?

I KILLED A MAN WITH AN EAR OF CORN. BUT I WAS PROVOKED.

HEY, LOOK! CORN FOR LUNCH. CAN YOU BELIEVE THAT?

DILBERT
By Scott Adams

I'VE HIRED A CONSULTANT TO CLARIFY OUR COMPANY POLICY ON DISCRIMINATION.

IT IS AGAINST POLICY TO DISCRIMINATE BASED ON RACE, SEX, AGE, HANDICAP OR RELIGION

CONSULTANT

DOES THAT INCLUDE UNPOPULAR, LITTLE RELIGIONS?

NO, THOSE ARE CONSIDERED CULTS; YOU MAY DISCRIMINATE FREELY AGAINST THEM.

WHAT ABOUT SHORT, BALD, FAT, UGLY MEN? ARE THEY CONSIDERED "HANDICAPPED"?

TECHNICALLY, NO. YOU CAN STILL TEASE THEM AND DENY THEM PROMOTIONS AS USUAL.

LIKEWISE, YOU MAY DISCRIMINATE AGAINST NERDS, SMOKERS, AND SINGLE PEOPLE.

AND WE'VE DROPPED "STUPID PEOPLE" FROM THE WATCH LIST, AS THEIR LOBBYING EFFORTS PROVED INEFFECTIVE...

DILBERT

By Scott Adams

Ratbert's Journal
Day one: I have disguised myself as a chihuahua so I can experience their lifestyle and make a movie.

I have already seen the senseless prejudice and brutality against an innocent chihuahua.

This morning I slapped myself with a rolled up newspaper for no apparent reason. It was strangely satisfying.

HEY, AREN'T YOU ONE OF THOSE CHIHUAHUA DOGS?

THE DISGUISE IS WORKING.

UNLESS... MAYBE YOU'RE JUST A RAT IN A TURTLENECK SWEATER, PRETENDING TO BE A CHIHUAHUA.

THINK FAST.

I DON'T HAVE THE ATTENTION SPAN TO THINK ABOUT IT.

WHAT DID HE MEAN BY "JUST A RAT"?

RATBERT! WHAT HAPPENED TO YOU?

MY CHIHUAHUA DISGUISE WORKED. I'VE BEEN TAUNTED AND CHASED ALL DAY BY BIGOTS WHO HATE CHIHUAHUAS FOR NO REASON.

THERE'S AN IMPORTANT LESSON IN THIS.

WHAT? CHIHUAHUAS ARE EVIL?

DILBERT

By Scott Adams

WOOOOOOOOOO

POLICE?

YOU MADE AN ILLEGAL U-TURN.

YOU'RE GIVING ME A TICKET FOR THAT?! A MEASLY U-TURN?!

I CAN'T BELIEVE IT! THE WORLD IS FULL OF MURDERERS AND THUGS, BUT YOU STOP ME?

I'M WASTING MY TAXES ON YOUR SALARY!

AND FRANKLY, THOSE MUSTACHES YOU GUYS ALL GROW DON'T MAKE YOU LOOK ANY SMARTER.

PLEASE STEP OUT OF YOUR CAR FOR THE SOBRIETY TEST.

© 1991 United Feature Syndicate, Inc.

7-21

...SO, IT TURNS OUT THAT THE SOBRIETY TEST INVOLVES FLINGING YOURSELF DOWN A MUDDY EMBANKMENT.

I'VE DECIDED TO ENTER THE STAND-UP COMEDY COMPETITION NEXT WEEK.

THE RULES SEEM PRETTY STRAIGHTFORWARD... FIVE MINUTES PER PERSON... THE FIRST MINUTE IS FREESTYLE COMEDY.

THE REMAINING TIME IS FOR THE MANDATORY CATEGORIES: DAN QUAYLE, FLATULENCE, AND THE WARNING LABELS ON MATTRESSES.

WHAT MAKES YOU THINK YOU CAN WIN THE STAND-UP COMEDY COMPETITION?

IT'S JUST A MATTER OF WRITING GOOD JOKES.

HERE'S ONE — "WHY DO WOMEN GO TO THE RESTROOM IN PAIRS?"

WHY?

BECAUSE THEY'RE STAPLED TO THE CHICKEN! HEE-HEE!

IT'S BEEN NICE KNOWING YOU.

DILBERT ENTERS A STAND-UP COMEDY COMPETITION.

IS THIS YOUR FIRST TIME?

YEAH.

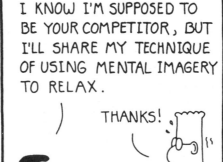

I KNOW I'M SUPPOSED TO BE YOUR COMPETITOR, BUT I'LL SHARE MY TECHNIQUE OF USING MENTAL IMAGERY TO RELAX.

THANKS!

IMAGINE THAT YOU'RE NAKED... AND THE AUDIENCE IS FULL OF MARY KAY SALES PEOPLE WITH CAMCORDERS...

HOW DID YOU DO IN THE STAND-UP COMEDY COMPETITION?

I WAS HALFWAY THROUGH MY FIRST JOKE -- ABOUT OLD PEOPLE, WHEN AN ELDERLY WOMAN DRAGGED ME OFF STAGE AND SLAPPED THE BEJEEZUS OUT OF ME.

...IT WAS GOOD ENOUGH FOR THIRD PLACE.

WILL YOU SIGN MY PETITION?

WHAT'S IT FOR, BOB?

I DIDN'T HAVE ANY COMPLAINTS, SO IT JUST SAYS "D-UHH."

DEMOCRACY IS A WONDERFUL THING.

FORGOT MY KEYS.

I'LL HAVE TO SLAP MY FOREHEAD AND MUTTER WHEN I TURN AROUND, OTHERWISE I'LL LOOK SILLY.

TOO HARD.

SMACK

DILBERT

By Scott Adams

DOGBERT'S
FIND-A-FRIEND
SERVICE

I'D LIKE TO
FIND A FRIEND.

HAVE A
SEAT.

I NEED TO ASK A
FEW QUESTIONS, SO
I DON'T ACCIDENT-
ALLY MATCH YOU
WITH SOMEBODY WHO'S
TOO GOOD FOR YOU.

ONE: WHEN A FRIEND
DOESN'T RETURN A BORROWED
TOOL, DO YOU?
  A: MAKE SARCASTIC
    COMMENTS;
  B: BUY A NEW TOOL;
  C: SET A LETHAL TRAP.

C: SET A LETHAL TRAP.

7-28
S.Adams

LATER

I'M AFRAID YOU
HAVEN'T QUALIFIED FOR
A NORMAL FRIEND... I
COULD SET YOU UP WITH
SOMEBODY WHO'S NEW IN
TOWN, BUT IT WOULDN'T LAST.

THERE'S ONE OPTION...
TWO, IF YOU COUNT
GROWING SEA MONKEYS.

YES, I HATE SEA
MONKEYS TOO. WHO
ARE YOU?

I'VE DECIDED TO BECOME A POP PSYCHOLOGIST AND LECTURER.

MY THEORY IS THAT YOU CAN BLAME ALL OF YOUR PROBLEMS ON INVISIBLE PEOPLE.

7-29

THAT DOESN'T SOUND HEALTHY.

DON'T BLAME ME. TALK TO JUAN AND CINDY.

© 1991 United Feature Syndicate, Inc.

I'VE DECIDED TO BECOME A POP PSYCHOLOGIST. I NEED YOUR HELP TO MAKE MY LECTURE VIDEO.

YOU CAME TO THE RIGHT PLACE, BABE. FIRST, YOU NEED A NEW LOOK.

© 1991 United Feature Syndicate, Inc.

NICE TRY, BUT FRANKLY, THIS LOOK DIDN'T WORK TOO WELL FOR MADONNA EITHER.

7-30

WELCOME TO THE DOGBERT LECTURE SERIES ON GUILT.

7-31

IN THE NEXT HOUR, YOU WILL LEARN HOW TO COPE WITH GUILT THE DOGBERT WAY.

© 1991 United Feature Syndicate, Inc.

AND IF YOU DON'T, WELL, IT TURNS OUT I GET PAID ANYWAY.

YOU CAN FREE YOUR-SELF FROM GUILT WITH THE COPYRIGHTED DOGBERT METHOD.

MY METHOD IS SO SIMPLE THAT EVEN STUPID PEOPLE CAN DO IT.

DO WE HAVE ANY STUPID PEOPLE HERE TODAY?

THE DOGBERT METHOD OF ELIMINATING GUILT IS QUITE SIMPLE.

ALL OF YOUR PROBLEMS ARE CAUSED BY INVISIBLE PEOPLE NAMED JUAN AND CINDY.

ALL YOU HAVE TO DO IS FIND THEM AND KILL THEM.

I FEEL LIKE I'M BEING JUDGED BY EVERYBODY I SEE.

WHY CAN'T PEOPLE ACCEPT OTHER PEOPLE AS THEY ARE, WITHOUT JUDGING THEM?

IT WAS A GOOD SPEECH, BUT IT LACKED EMOTION.

7.5

DILBERT

By Scott Adams

UH-OH... THAT GUY IS COMING TO TALK TO US.

I HATE THIS LONG WALK ACROSS THE ROOM.

YOU'RE THE UGLY ONE, EDNA. YOU'LL HAVE TO PROTECT ME.

THEY SPOTTED ME. THEY'RE PLANNING A DEFENSE.

I'LL PUSH YOU BETWEEN US. YOU START BABBLING ABOUT YOUR CAT OR SOMETHING.

I CAN'T DO IT. I'LL VEER OFF AT THE LAST MINUTE...

NOW, EDNA!

IT'S HARD TO BE THE PRETTY ONE.

I HAVE A CAT NAMED BOOTS.

WHEN'S THE BABY DUE?

ANY MINUTE NOW.

THIS COMPANY HAS NO MATERNITY LEAVE POLICY, SO I'M GOING TO DELIVER BY THE XEROX MACHINE AND KEEP WORKING.

8-5

THAT DOESN'T SEEM FAIR.

YEAH, ESPECIALLY IF YOU NEED TO MAKE COPIES.

ALICE, I NOTICED YOU GAVE BIRTH BY THE XEROX MACHINE THIS MORNING...

WE DON'T HAVE A MATERNITY LEAVE POLICY HERE, BUT IF YOU NEED SOME TIME, I'M SURE WE CAN FIND SOMEBODY LESS FERTILE TO FILL YOUR JOB.

THANK YOU, SIR, BUT I DON'T EXPECT ANY SPECIAL TREATMENT.

8-6

ALICE, I'VE BEEN THINKING... SINCE YOUR BABY WAS BORN IN THE OFFICE, HAVE YOU CONSIDERED NAMING IT AFTER YOUR BOSS?

AS A MATTER OF FACT, I DID NAME HIM AFTER YOU.

WANT SOME MORE MILK, "BUTT HEAD"?

8-7

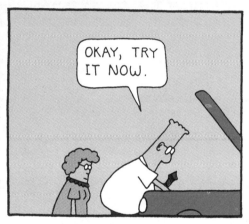

Panel 1:
DOGBERT THE USED CAR SALESMAN

I ASKED THE BOSS TO SELL IT AT YOUR PRICE.

Panel 2:
HE TOLD ME TO DRIVE OVER YOUR FOOT AND STEAL YOUR PURSE.

8-15

Panel 3:
BUT MAYBE I CAN CONVINCE HIM TO TAKE YOUR FIRST-BORN SON INSTEAD.

HE IS MY FIRST-BORN SON !!

Panel 4:
DOGBERT THE USED CAR SALESMAN.

HOW ABOUT THIS ONE?

Panel 5:
I DON'T WANT TO SPEND MUCH. I'M ONLY GOING TO TAKE IT APART AND LEAVE IT ON THE LAWN.

8-16

Panel 6:
I GOTTA BE ME.

Panel 7:
I QUIT MY JOB AS A USED CAR SALESMAN.

BECAUSE YOU COULDN'T KEEP LYING?

Panel 8:
NO, THE LYING WAS GOOD. I LIKED THAT PART.

WAS IT BECAUSE CRIME DOESN'T PAY?

Panel 9:
I MADE $400,000 THIS WEEK. I'M RETIRED NOW.

I DON'T THINK THIS WILL EVER BE A "READER'S DIGEST" VERY SPECIAL STORY.

8-17

DILBERT

By Scott Adams

COME HELP ME HOOK UP MY NEW VCR, DOGBERT.

YOU READ THE INSTRUCTIONS AND I'LL CONNECT THE CABLES.

"CONNECT THE 300 OHM TWIN-LEAD FLAT CABLE TO THE 75 OHM RF2 JACK."

"OR USE THE OPTIONAL 75 OHM CO-AXIAL CABLE WITH THE F TYPE CONNECTOR."

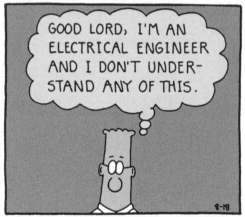

GOOD LORD, I'M AN ELECTRICAL ENGINEER AND I DON'T UNDER-STAND ANY OF THIS.

I'LL HAVE TO LIE TO THE OTHER ENGINEERS AND SAY I DON'T WANT TO RECORD TV SHOWS.

"NOW, STRIP NAKED, COVER YOUR BODY WITH MOTOR OIL AND RUN THROUGH TOWN YELLING WALLA-WALLA-WALLA."

LET ME SEE THAT.

"STEP SIX: DO NOT DOUBT THE NICE DOG."

S. Adams

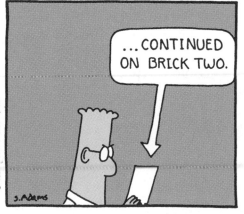

DILBERT, THIS IS YOUR NEW CO-WORKER, FLOYD REMORA.

FLOYD HAS WORKED HERE FOR TWENTY YEARS WITHOUT DEVELOPING ANY SKILLS. HE SURVIVES BY ATTACHING HIMSELF TO THE BACKS OF OTHER EMPLOYEES.

GO AHEAD... ASK ME HOW MY DAY WENT.

I SEE IT'S YOUR TURN TO WORK WITH FLOYD.

YEAH.

HE LIVED ON MY BACK FOR A YEAR, SHARING MY SUCCESSES WITHOUT CONTRIBUTING.

I HAD HIM LANCED.

DOES IT LEAVE A BIG HICKEY?

I DON'T MEAN TO SOUND CRITICAL ON A FIRST DATE, BUT THERE'S A LITTLE MAN ATTACHED TO YOUR BACK.

THAT'S FLOYD. HE'S A CO-WORKER WHO SURVIVES BY SHARING THE SUCCESS OF OTHERS.

WHAT IF YOU'RE NOT SUCCESSFUL?

HE'LL DIE. BUT HEY, NO PRESSURE.

55

DILBERT

By Scott Adams

Is this the meeting?

Mumble mumble

Good

Everybody take a copy of the agenda.

I'm in the wrong meeting... now it's too awkward to leave.

I'll casually stretch my arms, flick the lights off and escape under cover of dark.

Ouch! Ouch! Ouch!

Oh, sorry, wrong agenda.

I'm starting to think that the problem with our economy is deeper than high interest rates.

DILBERT

By Scott Adams

DILBERT: DOGBERT, THIS IS MY NEW CO-WORKER, JOHN SMITH.

DOGBERT: YO

JOHN SMITH: YO

DILBERT: I INVITED HIM OVER TO WATCH TELEVISION. HE DOESN'T HAVE CABLE YET.

TV: NEXT ON "AMERICA'S MOST WANTED."

TV: THIS MAN GAVE "WEDGIES" TO AN ENTIRE TOWN, ONE PERSON AT A TIME.

ALias: JOHN SMITH

TV: THE VICTIMS WERE WEDGIED IN THEIR OWN HOMES, USUALLY WHILE WATCHING THIS SHOW.

JOHN SMITH: CAN YOU LEAN OVER AND ADJUST THAT PICTURE?

DILBERT: SURE.

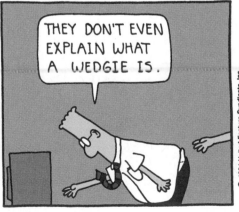

DILBERT: THEY DON'T EVEN EXPLAIN WHAT A WEDGIE IS.

DILBERT: THIS IS EXACTLY WHY I DON'T INVITE PEOPLE OVER MORE OFTEN.

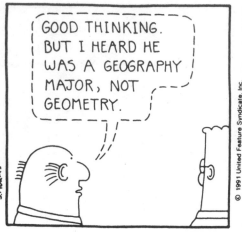

DILBERT

By Scott Adams

DILBERT

By Scott Adams

PSST...

WANT TO BUY A NUCLEAR BOMB?

HOW MUCH?

TWENTY BUCKS.

DEAL.

© 1991 United Feature Syndicate, Inc.

DOES THE GOVERNMENT KNOW ABOUT THIS?

I AM THE GOVERN-MENT.

IT'S THE ONLY WAY WE COULD AGREE ON TO REDUCE THE NATIONAL DEBT... YOU WOULDN'T BELIEVE HOW MANY OF THESE THINGS WE HAVE.

I'M GLAD I GOT MINE BEFORE SOME LIBERAL HAS A HISSY FIT.

10-6

DILBERT LANDS IN ELBONIA WITHOUT HIS SUITCASE.

SPLOIT

YOU BAGGED A NICE PIECE OF LUGGAGE, M'LORD.

I LIKE TO THINK THIS HELPS MAINTAIN THE DELICATE BALANCE OF NATURE.

YES, SIRE.

I'VE GOT TO CONVINCE HIM TO RESIGN.

KING DOGBERT

I FOUND HIM LURKING, SIRE. THE USUAL PUNISHMENT?

DILBERT!

DOGBERT!

WHAT IS THE USUAL PUNISH-MENT?

A BLIND DATE WITH "EDNA THE LONELIEST HUN."

YOU'VE GOT TO STEP DOWN AS KING OF ELBONIA. THESE PEOPLE ARE CAPABLE OF MAKING THEIR OWN DECISIONS.

THE PAPER-ROCK-SCISSORS OLYMPICS ARE CANCELED. WE COULDN'T AGREE ON THE RULES.

AND OF COURSE, WE ALL WEAR MITTENS...

WHAT WAS YOUR POINT?

DILBERT

By Scott Adams

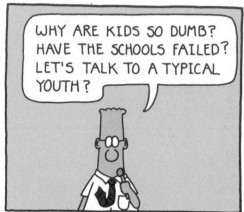

WHY ARE KIDS SO DUMB? HAVE THE SCHOOLS FAILED? LET'S TALK TO A TYPICAL YOUTH?

WHO WAS THE SIXTH PRESIDENT OF THE UNITED STATES?

WHO CARES?

HOW WILL HE EVER GET A JOB WITHOUT THIS BASIC KNOWLEDGE?

WHAT IS THE DEEPEST LAKE IN NORTH AMERICA?

WHO CARES?

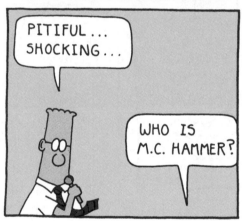

PITIFUL... SHOCKING...

WHO IS M.C. HAMMER?

I DON'T KNOW, BUT IT'S NOT IMPORTANT. IT'S TRIVIA.

OH, I SEE. WHAT YOU KNOW IS IMPORTANT, BUT WHAT I KNOW IS TRIVIA. YES, YES, IT ALL MAKES SENSE NOW.

IS THAT SARCASM?

D-UHH.

DILBERT

By Scott Adams

Dilbert: LOOK! A BEAUTIFUL REGENCY BUTTERFLY!

Dogbert: BEAUTIFUL?? IT'S A FLYING BUG.

Dilbert: IT MAY NOT SEEM LIKE MUCH NOW...

Dilbert: BUT AFTER WE KILL IT, DIP IT IN CHEMICALS, AND FLATTEN IT BETWEEN GLASS, IT BECOMES A BEAUTIFUL WORK OF ART!

Dogbert: DO WE THROW AWAY THE BUG GUTS AND JUST KEEP THE WINGS?

Dilbert: NO. THE GUTS KEEP THE WINGS EVENLY SPACED.

EEOW!!!
ANTS IN MY PANTS!!

© 1991 United Feature Syndicate, Inc.

MOTHER NATURE!

HE WAS STANDING RIGHT ON AN ANTHILL. I COULDN'T RESIST.

UH... WALLY, YOU'RE WEARING ONLY UNDERWEAR AT WORK.

I'M TRYING TO GET FIRED.

THE COMPANY LAYOFF PLAN IS VERY GENEROUS. I'LL GET A BIG PILE OF MONEY IF THEY ASK ME TO LEAVE.

THIS HAS GIVEN ME A DEGREE OF FREEDOM IN DEALING WITH LOCAL MANAGEMENT.

ANY LUCK TRYING TO GET FIRED?

NO... BUT I'LL GET THAT SEVERANCE PACKAGE YET.

THIS MORNING I KRAZY-GLUED FARM ANIMALS TO THE BOSS, BUT HE STILL WON'T DEAL WITH ALL THE BUREAUCRACY TO FIRE ME.

THE STAFF MEETING MAY RUN A LITTLE LONG TODAY.

I HAVEN'T LOOKED AT MY HIGH SCHOOL YEARBOOK IN AGES.

THERE'S MIKE — VOTED MOST LIKELY TO SUCCEED... AND LUCY — VOTED MOST BEAUTIFUL...

WHERE ARE YOU?

DILBERT — "MOST LIKELY TO FIND A POTATO THAT RESEMBLES HIMSELF."

WHO HASN'T?

THIS HIGH SCHOOL YEARBOOK REALLY BRINGS BACK THE MEMORIES.

THERE'S DOPEY BOBBY NOOBER. EVERY DAY WE'D TIE HIM TO THE FLAGPOLE AND STUFF LIVE FROGS IN HIS PANTS.

WHERE IS HE NOW?

HE'S STILL THE PRINCIPAL... NOT THE HAPPIEST GUY I'VE EVER KNOWN.

WE'VE GOT TO FOCUS MORE ON THE NEEDS OF OUR CUSTOMERS.

I'VE HIRED FAMOUS BUSINESS CONSULTANT TOM PETERS TO FOLLOW YOU AROUND AND MAKE PASSIONATE CRITICISM.

IS THIS QUALITY? ARE YOU TRULY FOCUSED ON THE CUSTOMER?

GREAT... HE'S A SPITTER.

I HAVE NO LUCK.

YOU KNOW WHAT THEY SAY, "IF LIFE GIVES YOU LEMONS, MAKE LEMONADE."

I'M ALLERGIC TO CITRUS.

YOU KNOW WHAT THEY SAY, "IF LIFE GIVES YOU LEMONS, SWELL UP AND DIE."

DILBERT

By Scott Adams

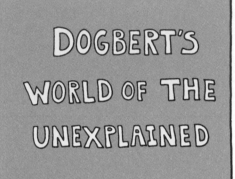

DOGBERT'S WORLD OF THE UNEXPLAINED

I'M AT THE FARM OF KAY AND CLEM BOVINSKI...

...THE LOCATION OF UNEXPLAINED PHENOMENA.

(DEEP VOICE) THE DISTURBANCES HAVE LASTED 40 YEARS

OBJECTS MOVE ALL BY THEMSELVES. SOMETIMES THEY HIT CLEM.

I RECKON IT'S POLTERGEIST. NO OTHER EXPLANATION MAKES SENSE.

BONK!

CUT.

DILBERT

By Scott Adams

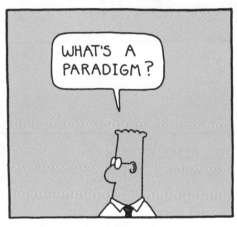

© 1991 United Feature Syndicate, Inc.

SOMEBODY LEFT A PENCIL IN THE ELECTRIC SHARPENER.

THAT'S "EXCALIBERT."

LEGEND HAS IT THAT WHOEVER CAN REMOVE EXCALIBERT FROM THE SHARPENER WILL BECOME CEO.

LIKE THIS?

CONTINUED...

YOU DID IT! YOU REMOVED THE PENCIL "EXCALIBERT" FROM THE SHARPENER.

AS CORPORATE LEGEND REQUIRED, DILBERT BECAME CEO.

HE IMMEDIATELY SET ABOUT THE TASK OF MAKING IMPORTANT DECISIONS.

HERE'S THE LIST OF PEOPLE WHO DIDN'T GROVEL SUFFICIENTLY.

NOW THAT I'M C E O WHAT AM I SUPPOSED TO ACTUALLY DO?

YOU'RE SUPPOSED TO MAKE SUPERFICIAL STATEMENTS ABOUT HOW GOOD THE COMPANY IS, THEN HOPE SOMETHING LUCKY HAPPENS AND PROFITS GO UP.

IT'S CALLED LEADERSHIP, SIR.

MAKE IT SO.

DILBERT

By Scott Adams

BOOK SIGNING TODAY

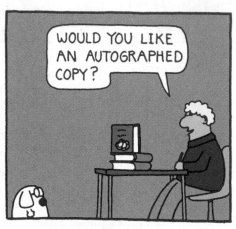

WOULD YOU LIKE AN AUTOGRAPHED COPY?

WHO ARE YOU?

I'M BOBBY MCNEWTON, CHILD-STAR FROM THE SIXTIES. I ONCE HAD A SPEAKING PART ON "LEAVE IT TO BEAVER."

I'M LEVERAGING MY FAME TO PROMOTE MY RECIPE BOOK.

Bobby McNewton's Cooking With Walnuts

"WALNUTS AND MILK: CRUSH WALNUTS ON TABLE. POUR MILK ON WALNUTS. SERVE COLD."

"WALNUTS AND PORK: KILL A PIG. COOK DEAD PIG. SPRINKLE WALNUTS ON PIG'S CORPSE."

11-10

I USED A GHOST WRITER.

WAS HE A GHOST BEFORE HE ATE YOUR FOOD?

DILBERT

By Scott Adams

LOOK, DOGBERT-- A WALLET.

IT'S FULL OF MONEY.

WE'RE RICH!!

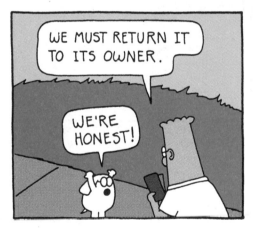

WE MUST RETURN IT TO ITS OWNER.

WE'RE HONEST!

HIS BUSINESS CARD SAYS "SAM GROOPER, RUTHLESS CRIMINAL."

LET'S HOPE "RUTHLESS" MEANS HE DIVORCED HIS WIFE NAMED RUTH.

MR. GROOPER, WE FOUND YOUR WALLET. NO REWARD IS EXPECTED.

HAND IT OVER. GIVE ME YOUR WALLET TOO. THEN SLAP YOURSELVES AROUND AND SCRAM.

WE'RE MORONS!

MISTER PRESIDENT, THERE'S ANOTHER OPENING ON THE SUPREME COURT. ONE OF THE OLD GUYS WANDERED AWAY.

I RECOMMEND NOMINATING A DOG THIS TIME. THEY TEND TO BE LOYAL AND EVERYBODY LIKES THEM.

11-25

IT'S FOR YOU... GEORGE SOME- BODY.

TAKE A MESSAGE.

MISTER DOGBERT, THE SENATE JUDICIARY COMMITTEE WILL BEGIN THE QUESTIONING.

HOW WOULD YOU INTERPRET ROE VERSUS WADE?

THEY'RE LYING. I DENY EVERYTHING.

11-26

WE'RE NOT ACCUSING YOU...

HEY, I DIDN'T BRING IT UP!

DOGBERT'S SUPREME COURT NOMINATION HEARINGS

DO YOU HAVE ANY OPINIONS ON THE RIGHT TO PRIVACY?

NO. IN FACT, I'VE NEVER FORMED AN IMPORTANT OPINION IN MY ENTIRE LIFE.

11-27

YOU MUST THINK WE'RE IDIOTS.

OKAY, I'VE FORMED ONE OPINION... BUT THAT'S ALL.

91

DILBERT
By Scott Adams

BOB THE DINOSAUR
RIPS THE PANTS
OFF OF GUYS
WE HATE FOR NO REASON

YES!

GUYS WHO WEAR THOSE LITTLE HELMETS TO RIDE A BICYCLE.

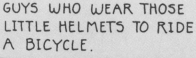

DID A 100 "K" TODAY.

AAAAGH!!

SAFETY FIRST!

RIP

GUYS WHO KNOW ACTUAL DANCE STEPS.

WOMEN LOVE THAT STUFF!

AAAGH!

GUYS WHO KNOW WINE.

FRUITY, YET TANNIC...

FLOWERY, YET POLYESTER!!

GUYS WHO CAN STOP A CONVERSATION COLD.

THAT REMINDS ME OF TRELLIS CODE MODULATION.

DILBERT

By Scott Adams

'TWAS THE NIGHT BEFORE CHRISTMAS...

WHEN A DUCK HIT THE SLED...

SMACK

SANTA FELL OUT...

AND DROPPED ON HIS HEAD...

HE WAS BARELY ALIVE, THIS JOLLY OLD ELF...

'TWAS THE HOLIDAY SEASON, SO I THOUGHT OF MYSELF...

HEY! I DON'T SEE ANY GIFTS HERE!

SO I STOLE HIS HAT AND BURIED HIM IN THE BACK YARD. THE END.

UH...THIS IS INTERESTING, DOGBERT.

THE SEQUEL IS TITLED "ELF WARS: THE TASTE OF VENISON."

12-22

WHAT DID YOU MEAN WHEN YOU SAID ALL EMPLOYEES ARE EMPOWERED?

DOES THAT MEAN I CAN CONTROL MY OWN BUDGET, MAKE DECISIONS WITHOUT TWELVE LEVELS OF APPROVAL, AND TAKE CALCULATED RISKS ON MY OWN?

NO, IT'S JUST A WAY TO BLAME EMPLOYEES FOR NOT DOING THE THINGS WE TELL THEM NOT TO DO.

NO WONDER YOU NEEDED A NEW WORD.

I'M USING A NEW SYSTEM FOR EVALUATING MY DATES. I JUST CHECK OFF BOXES ON THIS CARD THROUGHOUT THE NIGHT.

THERE... I JUST DINGED YOU A POINT FOR THAT NERVOUS TWITCH.

WOULD YOU SAY YOUR HEAD IS MORE LIKE A BLOCK OR A BUCKET?

DO YOU EVER WONDER ABOUT THE MEANING OF LIFE, DOGBERT?

I USED TO.

BUT I LOOKED IT UP IN THE DICTIONARY UNDER "L" AND THERE IT WAS – THE MEANING OF LIFE.

IT WAS LESS THAN I EXPECTED.

DID YOU TRY THE THESAURUS?

DILBERT

By Scott Adams

I'VE BEEN ASKED TO BRIEF EVERYBODY ON THE COMPANY'S POLICY FOR PROTECTING SECRET INFORMATION.

ALL SECRET INFORMATION MUST BE LOCKED UP AT NIGHT.

OUR SECRETS COULD BE OF GREAT VALUE TO OUR COMPETITORS.

IN FACT, SOME COMPANIES TRY TO BUY THE SECRETS OF THEIR COMPETITORS.

JUST OUT OF CURIOSITY, HOW MUCH WOULD OUR COMPETITORS PAY FOR OUR SECRETS?

OH, I DUNNO... MAYBE SEVERAL TIMES YOUR ANNUAL SALARY.

I DON'T THINK THIS WAS SOME OF MY BEST WORK.

© 1991 United Feature Syndicate, Inc.

RATBERT, I WANT YOU TO WEAR A DISGUISE AND INFILTRATE THE ELF GANG THAT HAS BEEN BOTHERING US.

CHECK

WE HAVEN'T SEEN YOU BEFORE...

WHAT'S THE SECRET HAND-SHAKE?

NO, BUT THAT'S ONE HECKUVA GOOD GUESS.

"WE THE ELVES MAKE THE FOLLOWING DEMANDS..."

WOULDN'T IT BE FUNNY IF I JUST SLAPPED YOUR POINTY HATS FLAT?

I CANNOT BELIEVE WHAT PASSES FOR FUNNY AROUND HERE.

WHEN YOU'RE NORTH OF THE EQUATOR, WATER SWIRLS CLOCKWISE DOWN THE DRAIN...

SOUTH OF THE EQUATOR, IT SWIRLS COUNTER-CLOCKWISE.

WHAT'S IT DO RIGHT ON THE EQUATOR?

ON THE EQUATOR

JUAN! IT'S JUST SITTING THERE AGAIN!

DILBERT

By Scott Adams

THANKS FOR AGREEING TO BABY-SIT, DOGBERT.

NO SWEAT.

DOGGIE-BERT!

SIT DOWN, BRET.

YOU'RE IN YOUR MOST INNOCENT AND IMPRESSIONABLE YEARS.

AS AN ADULT, IT IS MY DUTY TO FILL YOUR SPONGE-LIKE BRAIN WITH INCREDIBLE NONSENSE FOR MY OWN ENTERTAINMENT.

YOUR PARENTS ARE REALLY SPACE ALIENS.

THEY'RE JUST FATTENING YOU UP SO THEY CAN EAT YOU!

THE SLAUGHTER-HOUSE IS A PLACE THEY CALL KINDERGARTEN!!

THANKS, DOGBERT. DID YOU CHANGE HIM?

PROBABLY.

DILBERT

By Scott Adams

UNCLE NED, CAN WE SEE YOUR HUNTING TROPHIES AFTER DINNER?

OOOH...

I BAGGED THIS ONE AT THE ZOO.

THE ZOO? THAT'S ILLEGAL.

NO WONDER EVERYBODY GOT SO EXCITED.

THESE ARE SOME DOVES I KILLED WITH HELP FROM MY LOYAL DOG, RUSTY.

THAT'S RUSTY.

WE RAN OUT OF DOVES...

THESE WERE MY NEIGHBORS — FLORENCE, DAVE AND MUFFIN.

HEY, LOOK AT THE TIME! GOT TO RUN!

DON'T YOU WANT TO SEE MY "HALL-O'-POSTAL EMPLOYEES"?

NEW RULE: FIND OUT THEIR HOBBIES BEFORE YOU EAT THEIR POT ROAST.

WE SHOULD HAVE STAYED FOR THE "HALL-O'-POSTAL EMPLOYEES."

I THOUGHT YOU WERE MY FRIEND, RATBERT. WHY DID YOU TIP OFF THE AUTHORITIES ABOUT MY INSIDER STOCK TRADING?

I WAS AFRAID THAT IF YOU KEPT THE MONEY YOU WOULD LEAVE AND I'D NEVER SEE YOU AGAIN.

REALLY? GEE...

DID THEY GIVE YOU A REWARD?

YEAH, I'M OUTTA HERE!

I FIND YOU GUILTY OF STEALING MILLIONS IN AN INSIDER TRADING SCHEME.

LET'S SEE... ACCORDING TO MY SLIDING SCALE OF JUSTICE, THE PUNISHMENT AT YOUR INCOME IS... HMM...

I'M SENTENCED TO BE THE SUBJECT OF A KITTY KELLY BIOGRAPHY.

WHAT HAPPENED TO YOU?

KITTY KELLY WAS HERE TO WRITE YOUR BIOGRAPHY. SHE WAS ALL OVER ME. I THINK SHE TOOK MY WATCH.

I NEVER TRUST ANYBODY NAMED "KITTY."

I THINK I LOVE HER.

DILBERT
By Scott Adams

I HAVE A SOLUTION FOR YOUR DATING DILEMMA.

AT YOUR AGE THERE ARE MORE SINGLE MEN THAN SINGLE WOMEN.

WORSE YET, ALL OF THE SINGLE WOMEN ARE DATING MARRIED MEN OR SERIAL KILLERS.

BUT THE STATISTICS EVENTUALLY FAVOR MEN.

REALLY? HOW?

AT AGE 80 THERE ARE THREE TIMES AS MANY AVAILABLE WOMEN AS MEN BECAUSE MEN DIE YOUNGER.

ARE YOU SAYING I SHOULD WAIT UNTIL I'M OLD... AND DATE 80-YEAR-OLD WOMEN?

© 1992 United Feature Syndicate, Inc.

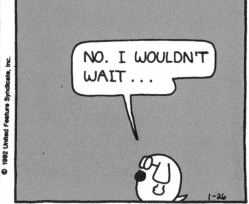

NO. I WOULDN'T WAIT...

1-26

DILBERT By Scott Adams

DILBERT! DOGBERT!

THANKS FOR INVITING US OVER.

WE THOUGHT YOU'D LIKE TO SEE OUR HOME VIDEO OF LITTLE TIMMY'S BIRTH.

WE CAPTURED EVERY BEAUTIFUL MOMENT ON VHS!

HAVE YOU EVER SEEN A CAESAREAN SECTION BEFORE?

THE DOCTOR IS MAKING THE INCISION!

NOW THEY'RE REMOVING THE SQUIGGLY THING!

WAIT... THIS MIGHT BE THE WRONG TAPE... I THINK THIS IS YOUR APPENDECTOMY VIDEO.

EITHER THAT OR LITTLE TIMMY ISN'T VERY PHOTOGENIC.

WHAT HAPPENED WITH THE ROBOT YOU WERE BUILDING?

NOBODY CAN MAKE A ROBOT. IT'S IMPOSSIBLE.

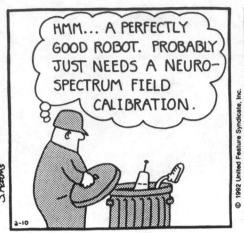

HMM... A PERFECTLY GOOD ROBOT. PROBABLY JUST NEEDS A NEURO-SPECTRUM FIELD CALIBRATION.

THAT WHOLE ROBOT PROJECT WAS BAD FOR MY EGO AS AN ENGINEER.

HEY! GUESS WHO'S _WAY_ SMARTER THAN YOU!

REMEMBER, THE "ROBOT'S CODE" REQUIRES YOU TO USE YOUR VAST STRENGTH TO SERVE, PROTECT, AND NEVER HARM HUMANS.

HA! I DIDN'T SIGN ANY "ROBOT'S CODE." IN FACT, WITH MY VAST STRENGTH I CAN MAKE _YOU_ SERVE _ME_!

I FORGOT TO PROGRAM IN THE "ROBOT'S CODE."

MAYBE I'LL CRUSH YOUR HEAD JUST FOR FUN!

I MADE SOME PANTS OUT OF THE CLOTHES IN YOUR DRESSER.

BAD ROBOT!! I WANT YOU TO TELL ME WHY WHAT YOU DID WAS WRONG.

IT'S NOT WRONG. I REMEMBERED TO MAKE UNDERPANTS OUT OF THE DRAPES.

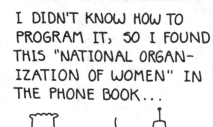

DILBERT

By Scott Adams

BANK OF ETHEL

NOW A SECRET SWISS BANK

I'D LIKE TO WITHDRAW TWO HUNDRED DOLLARS.

WHAT'S YOUR SECRET SWISS ACCOUNT NUMBER?

I DON'T HAVE A SECRET ACCOUNT. IT'S JUST A REGULAR ACCOUNT.

WRONG. I CHANGED ALL OF THE ACCOUNTS INTO SECRET SWISS ACCOUNTS.

OH, OKAY, WHAT'S MY SECRET ACCOUNT NUMBER?

IT'S A SECRET.

THEN HOW DO I GET MY MONEY OUT?

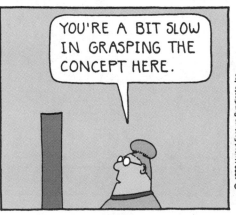

YOU'RE A BIT SLOW IN GRASPING THE CONCEPT HERE.

OKAY, OKAY I'LL JUST OPEN A NEW ACCOUNT.

DO YOU HAVE ANY PREVIOUS BANKING REFERENCES?

RATBERT, I'M LOOKING FOR A VICE PRESIDENT FOR MY TICKET.

I NEED SOMEBODY WHO IS SO INEPT AND SIMPLE-MINDED THAT I ALWAYS LOOK GOOD IN COMPARISON.

I DON'T UNDERSTAND.

OKAY, OKAY, YOU'VE GOT THE JOB.

SURE, DOGBERT, I'LL BE YOUR ELECTION CAMPAIGN STRATEGIST.

YOU CAN WIN IF YOU PROMISE TO SELL OUR NATIONAL PARKS TO FOREIGNERS AND SHARE THE PROFITS.

I COULDN'T DO THAT.

YOU COULDN'T SELL THE PARKS?

I COULDN'T SHARE THE PROFITS.

THE KEY TO WINNING THE ELECTION IS VOTER TURNOUT.

TO BE SPECIFIC, YOU WANT EVERYBODY TO STAY HOME EXCEPT YOU.

I'VE WORKED UP A LITTLE AD CAMPAIGN.

HE TOUCHED THE VOTING BOOTH BEFORE YOU DID.

AND HE NEVER WASHES HIS HANDS

DILBERT

By Scott Adams

DOGBERT PRESENTS

THE SEVEN ADVANTAGES OF BEING DUMB

#1. IMPENDING DOOM DOESN'T BOTHER YOU
THERE'S A HOLE IN THE OZONE LAYER.
COOL!

#2. TELEVISION IS A SOURCE OF CONSTANT WONDER
I WONDER IF DOOGIE IS A DOCTOR IN REAL LIFE.

#3. YOU HAVE A SOLUTION FOR EVERY PROBLEM
IF PEOPLE ARE STARVING IN AFRICA THEY SHOULD MOVE TO FRANCE.

#4. YOU ARE NOT CONSTRAINED BY A BUDGET
IT WAS FREE! THEY JUST MAKE YOU SIGN PAPERS!

#5. YOU'VE SEEN ELVIS. FREQUENTLY.
IT'S THE KING!

#6. INSTANT REPLAYS ARE AS EXCITING AS LIVE ACTION.
THIS TIME HE COULD MAKE IT.

#7. YOU RECEIVE TWICE AS MANY COMPLIMENTS.
YOU'RE KIND OF THE DAN QUAYLE OF DINOSAURS.
REALLY?! WOW!

3-1

132

THE POLL RESULTS ARE IN.

YOU STILL HAVE LOW NAME-RECOGNITION OUTSIDE OF THE LIVING ROOM... BUT SOME GUY IN THE KITCHEN THINKS HE'S HEARD OF YOU.

DON'T BE DISCOURAGED, UH...UH...

DOGBERT!

I'M GOING TO HOST MY OWN TELEVISION SHOW.

IT'S CALLED "DOGBERT'S WORLD OF AMAZINGLY IGNORANT PEOPLE."

OF COURSE, I'LL FILM YOU IN SHADOWS AND ALTER YOUR VOICE ELECTRON-ICALLY.

THAT'S VERY CONSIDERATE.

WELCOME TO DOGBERT'S WORLD OF AMAZINGLY IGNORANT PEOPLE.

TONIGHT WE'LL VISIT PEOPLE WHO DON'T UNDERSTAND ECONOMICS BUT TALK ABOUT IT ANYWAY.

SO, I HEARD THE FED INCREASED THE MONEY SUPPLY, BUT I CHECKED MY BANK BALANCE AND IT'S THE SAME AS BEFORE.

THAT ISN'T FAIR.

DILBERT

By Scott Adams

TAX PREPARATION $5 00

I NEED SOME HELP...

SIT DOWN.

I ALWAYS FOOLED AROUND DURING MATH CLASSES. NOW I CAN'T DO MY OWN TAXES.

WE CAN PRATTLE ABOUT YOUR INADEQUACIES LATER.

I'LL DO YOUR TAXES AND TALK AT THE SAME TIME SO YOU REALLY FEEL DUMB.

HMM... SIMPLY MULTIPLY THE STANDARD DEVIATION OF THE COSINE OF YOUR DEPRECIATION AND INTEGRATE THE RESULTING POLYNOMIAL... THERE.

ACCORDING TO THIS, YOU OWE YOUR TAX PREPARER AN ADDITIONAL TWO THOUSAND DOLLARS.

CONFUSION — IT WORKS FOR THE IRS AND IT CAN WORK FOR YOU.

MISTER DOGBERT, YOU MADE A GOOD ARGUMENT IN YOUR PETIMONY SUIT AGAINST DILBERT...

BUT DILBERT HAD SOME GOOD POINTS, TOO... I CALL IT A TIE.

THIRD TIE THIS WEEK ... MAYBE IT'S ME...

3-16

I'M NOT REALLY A GENIUS.

DID YOU SAY SOMETHING?

I'M PRACTICING MY FALSE HUMILITY.

IS THIS JUST A WAY TO WEASEL MORE COMPLIMENTS OUT OF PEOPLE?

OH, I COULD NEVER BE THAT CLEVER.

3-17

I'VE BEEN USING FALSE HUMILITY TO WEASEL COMPLIMENTS OUT OF PEOPLE...

BUT I KNOW YOU'RE WAY TOO SMART TO FALL FOR THAT TRICK, RATBERT.

3-18

ACTUALLY, I'M AS DUMB AS TOAST.

THEN I FOUND I COULD USE FALSE COMPLIMENTS TO MAKE PEOPLE INSULT THEMSELVES.

DILBERT
By Scott Adams

MY CODE NAME IS DOGBERT. I'M AN INDUSTRIAL SPY.

WHAT MAKES YOU THINK MY COMPANY NEEDS YOUR SERVICES?

IT'S PRETTY OBVIOUS THAT YOU WON'T SURVIVE ON YOUR WITS ALONE.

THERE'S A RUMOR THAT XYPON INC. IS DEVELOPING A TACTICAL NUCLEAR WEAPON TO USE AGAINST YOU.

WHAT EXACTLY WILL YOU DO FOR US?

YOU GIVE ME FIFTY THOUSAND DOLLARS, THEN I DISAPPEAR FOR A MONTH AND DO SECRET SPY THINGS.

I'LL RETURN WITH INFORMATION THAT ONLY A SPY OR A REGULAR NEWSPAPER READER COULD KNOW.

HOW GOOD ARE THEY, AGENT DOGBERT?

XYPON INC.

THEY'RE A BIT GULLIBLE.

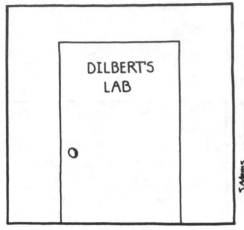

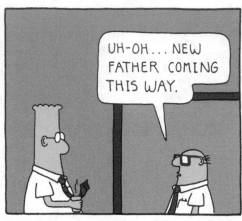

I'M GOING TO WASHINGTON TO BE AN ECONOMIC ADVISOR.

I'LL RECOMMEND A TAX REBATE FOR ALL DOGS. IT'S THE ONLY FAIR WAY TO STIMULATE THE ECONOMY.

3-30

SOUNDS LIKE A SELFISH PLOY TO LINE YOUR POCKETS AT THE EXPENSE OF OTHERS.

POTĀTO, PO-TAH-TO...

YOU'RE GOING TO BE AN ECONOMIC ADVISOR TO THE PRESIDENT? WHAT DO YOU KNOW ABOUT ECONOMICS?

IT'S SIMPLE, BOB.

THE COUNTRY NEEDS TO GIVE ALL THE MONEY TO DOGS, THUS STIMULATING THE ECONOMY.

3-31

WHY CAN'T WE SPEND THE MONEY OURSELVES?

YOU'D PROBABLY FRITTER IT AWAY ON FOOD AND HEALTH CARE.

SO, MISTER PRESIDENT, A TAX REBATE FOR DOGS IS THE ONLY FAIR WAY TO STIMULATE THE ECONOMY.

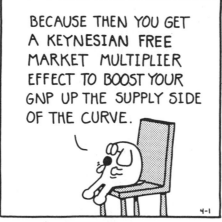

BECAUSE THEN YOU GET A KEYNESIAN FREE MARKET MULTIPLIER EFFECT TO BOOST YOUR GNP UP THE SUPPLY SIDE OF THE CURVE.

4-1

ARE YOU POSITIVE THAT DOGS CAN VOTE?

NOW, R-E-E-L HIM IN...

THE CANINE TAX REBATE BILL WAS PASSED BY CONGRESS TODAY.

THE BILL'S AUTHOR, MISTER DOGBERT, SUCCESSFULLY PINNED THE LABEL "DOG KICKING LIBERAL" ON ALL WHO OPPOSED HIM.

WAS THAT ETHICAL?

THA-A-AT'S IT. YOU'RE ON THE LIST.

...SO, THEN I THOUGHT, HA! MAYBE THERE'S A BUG IN THE COMPILER PROGRAM ITSELF!

AAAGH!

MAYBE THAT STORY WENT ON A LITTLE LONG...

WHAT GAVE IT AWAY?

HAVE YOU HEARD ABOUT THE IDAHO FLU THAT'S GOING AROUND?

AT FIRST YOU FEEL PERFECTLY HEALTHY... THEN BAM, YOU DIE.

HEY, I FEEL PERFECTLY HEALTHY RIGHT NOW.

MY WORK HERE IS DONE.

DILBERT

By Scott Adams

© 1992 United Feature Syndicate, Inc.

4-5

DILBERT

By Scott Adams

DOGBERT'S GUIDE TO MOVIE ADVERTISEMENTS

TRUST ME.

"THUMBS UP."

GENE SISKEL

MEANING: ROGER EBERT HATES IT.

"NOMINATED FOR AN ACADEMY AWARD."

NOTICE THEY DON'T SAY FOR WHAT-- PROBABLY "BEST GAFFER."

"FUNNIEST MOVIE OF THE YEAR."

HE SAW IT IN MID-JANUARY.

"☆☆☆☆...A MASTER-PIECE!"

THE MOVIE STUDIO ONLY PAID OFF ONE CRITIC. MUST BE A LOW-BUDGET FILM.

"POWERFUL PERFORMANCES."

IT'S A DOWNER. SOME-BODY PROBABLY GETS A DISEASE AND LOSES THE FARM.

"I LOVED IT!"

—FLOYD BELCHER, NOSEHAIR GAZETTE

REMEMBER TO CONSIDER THE SOURCE.

"STALLONE'S FUNNIEST MOVIE YET."

I THINK YOU GET THE HANG OF IT.

S.Adams

4-12

DILBERT

By Scott Adams

DOGBERT, COME LOOK AT OUR NEW CAR!

IT HAS ALL OF THE MOST IMPORTANT SAFETY FEATURES.

YOU GOT YOUR ANTI-LOCK BRAKES, YOUR REINFORCED BUMPERS, YOUR AUTOMATIC SEATBELTS AND YOUR DRIVER-SIDE AIR BAG.

I DIDN'T HEAR "PASSENGER SIDE AIR BAG" IN THAT LIST

IT TURNS OUT THAT IT'S ONLY ECONOMICAL TO SAVE THE PERSON WHO MAKES THE BUYING DECISION.

BUT I GOT A BABY SEAT IN CASE YOU WANT TO USE THAT.

WELL, THANK YOU FOR LETTING ME CHOOSE BETWEEN HUMILIATION AND DEATH.

I'VE GOT A BETTER IDEA.

OOH... JUST WAIT UNTIL MY TURN.

WATCH ME RAM THAT COP CAR.

AAAGH! YOU WHACKED RANDY WITH YOUR REMOTE CONTROL AIRPLANE !!!

—OOPS!

I'M WARNING YOU, FRISBEE PEOPLE AND AIRPLANE PEOPLE DON'T MIX... LIKE CATTLE AND SHEEP... YOU'LL PAY FOR THIS !! I SWEAR ...

4-23

GOOD ONE, DOGBERT.

MPHF! AACK! COUGH! HMP! GURGLE!

4-24

IF YOU'RE PRETENDING TO CHOKE TO DEATH TO END OUR DATE EARLY, IT WON'T WORK.

LIKE I HAVEN'T SEEN THAT TRICK A JILLION TIMES.

I'M HAVING A CRISIS OF SELF IMAGE.

4-25

DO I, AS A RAT, ADD ANY VALUE TO THE WORLD? OR DO I SIMPLY DEPLETE ITS RESOURCES, THEN DIE?

OH... SORRY... I SUCKED ALL THE MUSIC OUT OF THE ROOM.

DILBERT

By Scott Adams

© 1992 United Feature Syndicate, Inc.

YOU MUST RENOUNCE ALL PHYSICAL PLEASURE BEFORE YOU CAN ACHIEVE TRUE COSMIC JOY.

RENOUNCE IT?! HECK, I DON'T THINK I'VE EVER _HAD_ A PHYSICAL PLEASURE!

AND YOU MUST SHAVE YOUR HEAD...

OH, I GET IT; THEN YOU CAN RUB THE LITTLE STUBBLE AS IT GROWS IN!

© 1992 United Feature Syndicate, Inc.

TO REACH COSMIC JOY YOU MUST GIVE AWAY ALL OF YOUR POSSESSIONS.

WHAT IF I GIVE EVERY-THING AWAY BUT STILL DO NOT ACHIEVE COSMIC JOY?

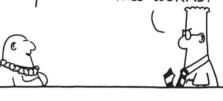

THEN THE COSMIC JOY IS ON YOU.

I'M STARTING TO SEE HOW THIS WORKS.

© 1992 United Feature Syndicate, Inc.

HERE'S MY REPORT. IT'S SOME OF MY BEST WORK.

BZZZZZZZT!

I HATE THAT PORTO-SHREDDER.

SAY, IS THAT A SILK NECKTIE?

© 1992 United Feature Syndicate, Inc.

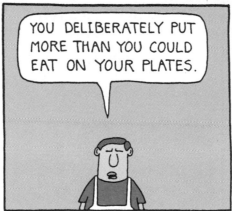

DILBERT

By Scott Adams

HOW CAN I TELL WHEN SPAGHETTI IS COOKED?

I'LL HAVE TO WEAR THE HAT TO ANSWER THAT QUESTION.

THE SPAGHETTI IS DONE WHEN YOU CAN THROW IT AT THE WALL AND MAKE IT STICK.

SEEMS ODD... BUT HE WAS WEARING THE HAT.

WHAP! SPLASH!

PREFERABLY, ONE STRAND AT A TIME.

DILBERT

By Scott Adams

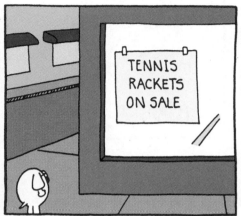

TENNIS RACKETS ON SALE

I'M LOOKING FOR A NEW RACKET.

YOU'RE PROBABLY INTERESTED IN OUR COLORFUL ALL-PLASTIC RACKETS FOR PATHETIC BEGINNERS.

NO, ACTUALLY I'M INTERESTED IN THE TITANIUM ALLOY DEATHSTICK 3000.

HA HA! AS IF A DUMPY LITTLE POOCH COULD HANDLE THAT KIND OF POWER ON THE COURT!

HERE... YOU CAN TOUCH IT, BUT I'M ONLY HUMORING YOU.

BOOM!

THIS IS THE PERFECT RACKET FOR THOSE WHO DON'T TAKE LOSING GRACEFULLY.

5-17

165

SOMETIMES I WONDER IF IT'S ETHICAL TO DO THESE GENETIC EXPERIMENTS.

BUT I RATIONALIZE IT BECAUSE IT WILL HELP IMPROVE THE QUALITY OF LIFE.

WHAT ARE YOU MAKING?

SKUNKOPOTAMUS.

5-25

I'LL USE DILBERT'S GENETIC LAB TO MAKE A MAN WITH THE WISDOM OF GHANDI AND THE STRENGTH OF WILT CHAMBERLAIN.

OR VICE-VERSA.

5-26

GIMME YOUR CAR KEYS. I'M GONNA FIND US SOME BABES.

NOT IN MY SHEET.

HELLO, LADIES.

I'M WILT GANDHI. I'M THE PRODUCT OF A GENETIC EXPERIMENT COMBINING THE WISDOM OF WILT CHAMBERLAIN AND THE BODY OF GANDHI.

5-27

THAT'S THE BEST LINE TONIGHT. I'M GOING FOR IT.

HEY, I SAW HIM FIRST.

DILBERT

By Scott Adams

THANKS FOR YOUR TIME, DILBERT. IT'S ALWAYS GOOD TO GET THE TECHNICAL PERSPECTIVE.

HEY, IT'S LUNCHTIME. WOULD YOU LIKE TO JOIN ME IN THE CAFETERIA?

OOH... NO, I COULDN'T DO THAT.

I'M ON THE MANAGEMENT TRACK, SO I CAN'T BE SEEN EATING LUNCH WITH YOU.

IF I'M SEEN WITH AN ORDINARY EMPLOYEE THEN PEOPLE WILL THINK I'M ORDINARY.

I'D LIKE TO EAT WITH THE SENIOR EXECUTIVES, BUT OF COURSE THEY DON'T WANT TO BE SEEN WITH ME.

SO I'VE PERFECTED A METHOD OF SLIPPING QUIETLY AWAY AT LUNCH TIME.

THE SCARY PART IS THAT SOMEDAY THAT MAN WILL BE MY BOSS.

5-31

NOBODY EVER CALLS ON MY NEW VIDEO PHONE SO I ROUTED THE TELEVISION SIGNAL TO IT.

NOW I CAN PRETEND THAT CELEBRITIES ARE CALLING ME ALL DAY.

OOH... DOLLY PARTON IS CALLING. I'LL BET IT'S FOR ME AGAIN.

ALL WEEK I'VE BEEN WATCHING VIOLENT MOVIES AT THE LAB.

A GROUP OF PARENTS ARE STUDYING ME TO SEE IF I BECOME INURED TO VIOLENCE.

ARE YOU?

YEAH. I'M PLANNING TO GNAW THE PARENTS TO DEATH TOMORROW.

I DON'T KNOW WHAT WE CAN DO TO MEET MORE MEN.

HI, MY NAME IS DILBERT.

GET LOST... I'M ARMED.

AND THE MEN WE DO MEET ALL HAVE THAT SAME STUNNED BUNNY LOOK.

DILBERT
By Scott Adams

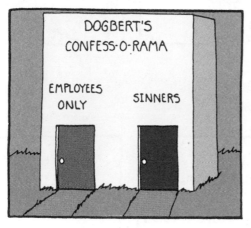

DOGBERT'S CONFESS-O-RAMA

EMPLOYEES ONLY

SINNERS

DOGBERT, I HAVE SINNED.

I WAS GOING TO MAKE CHOCOLATE CHIP COOKIES...

BUT I MADE THE MISTAKE OF TASTING A CHOCOLATE CHIP RIGHT FROM THE BAG.

BEFORE I KNEW IT, I HAD SCARFED THE ENTIRE BAG OF CHIPS!

FOR PENANCE YOU MUST MAKE A LITTLE DUNCE HAT FROM OLD "CATHY" COMIC STRIPS...

THEN WEAR THE LITTLE HAT WHILE DANCING NAKED ON YOUR LAWN WITH THE SPRINKLERS ON.

THANK YOU, DOGBERT.

IT'S SO REWARDING TO BE ABLE TO GIVE SOMETHING BACK TO THE COMMUNITY.

6-14

I'M PROUD TO ANNOUNCE THAT THE COMPANY HAS FOUND YET ANOTHER WAY TO DEHUMANIZE THE EMPLOYEES.

FROM NOW ON YOU WILL WEAR IDENTIFICATION BADGES AT WORK. THIS SYMBOLIZES THAT PEOPLE WHO LOOK LIKE YOU ARE OFTEN CRIMINALS.

6-18

OH... AND THE CAFETERIA IS CLOSED. WE'LL JUST LAY DOWN SOME ALFALFA IN THE BREAK ROOM.

© 1992 United Feature Syndicate, Inc.

MAYBE TED CAN ANSWER THAT QUESTION...

UH-OH

THEY'RE TRYING TO MAKE ME WORK. I'LL HAVE TO USE BODY LANGUAGE TO DISCOURAGE THEM.

6-19

UH... NEVER MIND

IT'S WORKING.

© 1992 United Feature Syndicate, Inc.

I'D LIKE TO APPLY FOR A "BANK OF ETHEL" CREDIT CARD.

SIT DOWN AND SHUT UP.

6-20

IT'S 21% INTEREST PLUS SURPRISINGLY HIGH ANNUAL FEES. WE'LL DO A CREDIT CHECK AND A FULL BODY CAVITY SEARCH.

© 1992 United Feature Syndicate, Inc.

...AND I HAD TO SMILE THE WHOLE TIME BECAUSE THEY WERE FILMING IT FOR THEIR TELEVISION ADS.

YOU HAVE TO ADMIRE THEIR ATTITUDE.

DILBERT

By Scott Adams

ANOTHER MASTERPIECE.

WHAT ARE YOU DOING, DOGBERT?

I DISCOVERED A HIGHLY EFFICIENT ART FORM.

I'VE BRILLIANTLY COMBINED THE SIMPLICITY OF CHARCOAL WITH THE SIMPLICITY OF ABSTRACT EXPRESSION.

THE SECRET IS TO LET YOUR DEEPEST INNER FEELINGS GUIDE THE CHARCOAL.

INNER FEELINGS?! WHAT INNER FEELINGS? THESE ARE SCRIBBLES.

ALL I SEE HERE IS THAT A CYNICAL DOG THINKS ART BUYERS ARE A BUNCH OF GULLIBLE MORONS.

WOW! I NAILED THAT ONE!

TELL ME WHAT YOU'VE ACCOMPLISHED THIS YEAR SO I CAN WRITE YOUR PERFORMANCE APPRAISAL.

THE INVENTIONS I MADE LAST YEAR -- THAT YOU THOUGHT WERE WORTHLESS, WILL GENERATE TWELVE MILLION IN LICENSE FEES NEXT YEAR!

SO, NO REAL ACCOMPLISHMENTS THIS YEAR?

I'M GOING TO OPEN A SCHOOL FOR PEOPLE WITH NO COMMON SENSE.

WHO WOULD PAY TO GO TO A SCHOOL THAT TEACHES SOMETHING THAT CAN'T BE LEARNED?

EXCEPT MAYBE PEOPLE WITH NO COMMON SENSE...

BINGO.

WELCOME TO DOGBERT'S SCHOOL OF COMMON SENSE.

I'VE ASKED YOU TO PAY TUITION IN ADVANCE; THAT WAY IF YOU'RE UNSATISFIED WITH THE SCHOOL, YOU'LL HAVE THE ADDED NEGOTIATING LEVERAGE OF HAVING ALREADY PAID.

AND THANKS, ALICE, FOR ASKING IF TIPPING IS CUSTOMARY.

Panel 1:

DOGBERT'S SCHOOL OF COMMON SENSE.

WHO CAN SHOW ME HOW TO GET THE WATER OUT OF THIS BOOT?

Panel 2:

IF YOU HAVE TROUBLE, THE DIRECTIONS ARE WRITTEN ON THE HEEL.

6-25

Panel 3:

I'M SORRY, BETTY. I CAN ONLY GIVE YOU PARTIAL CREDIT FOR TRYING TO ABSORB THE LIQUID WITH YOUR HAIR.

Panel 4:

DOGBERT'S SCHOOL OF COMMON SENSE.

TODD, SHOW THE CLASS HOW YOU HAND THESE SCISSORS TO RUSSELL.

6-26

Panel 5:

DON'T RUN! DON'T RUN!

AAAGH!

Panel 6:

SORRY, RUSSELL. IT'S THE TEACHER'S FAULT; HE DIDN'T EVEN ASK IF I NEED LEFT-HANDED SCISSORS.

Panel 7:

DOGBERT'S SCHOOL OF COMMON SENSE

THIS IS THE STORY OF CLAYTON THE AUTO MECHANIC.

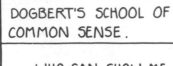

Panel 8:

CLAYTON SMOKED CIGARS WHILE WORKING ON GASOLINE ENGINES. WHAT PROBLEM DID THIS CAUSE?

BOOM

Panel 9:

HE WAS HIT BY LIGHTNING EVERY TIME?

DOES ANYBODY BESIDE CLAYTON HAVE A GUESS?

6-27

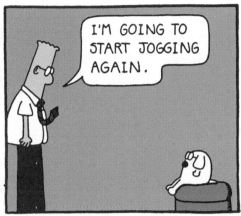

DILBERT

By Scott Adams

DILBERT, DO YOU HAVE A MINUTE?

THE COMPANY IS DOING A SURVEY OF EMPLOYEE ATTITUDES ABOUT THEIR BOSSES.

IT'S TOTALLY ANONYMOUS, SO YOU DON'T HAVE TO FEAR ANY RETRIBUTION.

OOPS! IT LOOKS LIKE YOUR QUESTIONAIRE IS A BIT DOG-EARED.

I'LL PUT MY PHONE NUMBER ON THE CONFIDENTIAL ENVELOPE IN CASE YOU NEED ME.

YOU CAN USE THIS GREEN MARKER PEN.

OH, AND I TOOK THE LIBERTY OF CHECKING OFF YOUR ETHNIC BACKGROUND AS ESKIMO. IT'S JUST A STATISTICAL THING.

1. DOES YOUR BOSS CLEARLY COMMUNICATE YOUR OBJECTIVES?

© 1992 United Feature Syndicate, Inc.

7-5

GEE, MARY, YOU WEREN'T WILLING TO DATE ME BEFORE I MADE MILLIONS IN THE STOCK MARKET.

I'M AFRAID YOU SEE ME AS JUST A BIG, TALKING WALLET.

YOU'RE MUCH MORE THAN THAT.

FOR EXAMPLE, YOU ALSO WEAR THICK GLASSES.

TOO LITTLE, TOO LATE.

I'VE BEEN MISERABLE SINCE I MADE MY FORTUNE IN THE STOCK MARKET...

IT'S THE "LAW OF FOUND MONEY." NATURE WON'T ALLOW US TO KEEP MONEY WE FIND ON THE GROUND OR WIN BY CHANCE. DON'T RESIST; LET YOUR INTUITION GUIDE YOU.

THIS COMES WITH A COLOR MONITOR, RIGHT?

GRAY 9

ONLY $10,000,000

I SPENT MY ENTIRE FORTUNE TO BUY THIS SUPERCOMPUTER.

WHAT DOES IT DO?

IT CAN CALCULATE THE VALUE OF PI TO ABOUT A JILLION DECIMAL PLACES...

A LOT OF PEOPLE TALK ABOUT THE AREAS OF CIRCLES, BUT I'M DOING SOMETHING ABOUT IT.

DILBERT

By Scott Adams

HEY, THAT'S MISS MULPUT, MY OLD FOURTH GRADE TEACHER.

HI, MISS MULPUT! DO YOU REMEMBER ME — DILBERT?

NO.

YOU USED TO MAKE ME WRITE ON THE BOARD A THOUSAND TIMES "I WILL NOT BE HOMELY IN CLASS."

OH, YEAH. THAT WAS A GOOD ONE.

AT THE TIME IT SEEMED LIKE PRETTY STRICT PUNISHMENT FOR CHEWING GUM.

BUT THAT EXPERIENCE MADE ME WHAT I AM TODAY...

AN ANGRY ADULT, OBSESSED WITH THOUGHTS OF REVENGE.

7-19

YOU KNOW, MISS "MOLEPIT," IF MY DOG HAD YOUR FACE I'D SHAVE HIS HINEY AND MAKE HIM WALK BACKWARD.

LEAVE ME OUT OF THIS.

DILBERT

By Scott Adams

NOW SHOWING
HANDS-OF-DEATH

Boycot

Boycot

WHY ARE YOU PROTESTING AGAINST THIS MOVIE?

Boycot

IT PORTRAYS RED HEADS AS HOT TEMPERED AND IGNORANT.

Boycot

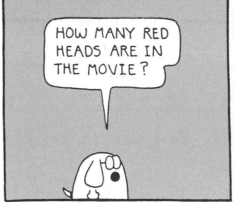

HOW MANY RED HEADS ARE IN THE MOVIE?

ONE. BUT THE POINT IS, RED HEADS DON'T FIT THEIR STEREOTYPE OF BEING HOT TEMPERED AND IGNORANT.

Boycot

ACTUALLY, IGNORANCE WAS NEVER A STEREOTYPE OF RED HEADS UNTIL YOU BROUGHT IT UP HERE.

7-26

SEAN, YOU IDIOT! I TOLD YOU!

SHUT UP, DENNIS! I'LL POUND YOU TO A PULP!!

Boycot

Boycot

AND "BOYCOTT" IS SPELLED WITH A DOUBLE "T."

DILBERT

By Scott Adams

NATURE IS SO WONDERFUL...

S. Adams

THEY SAY WE DON'T LEAVE THE PLANET TO FUTURE GENERATIONS, WE BORROW IT FROM OUR CHILDREN.

IT'S EVEN BETTER THAN THAT.

WE DON'T HAVE CHILDREN, SO WE'RE BORROWING THE PLANET FROM COMPLETE STRANGERS!

AND THERE'S NO COLLATERAL. WE CAN USE UP THE PLANET, HAVE GREAT LIVES AND LEAVE AN EMPTY SMOKING SHELL TO THE STRANGERS!

I TELL YOU, PEOPLE HAVE COMPLETELY OVERLOOKED THE POSITIVE SIDE OF THIS ENVIRONMENT SITUATION.

8-2

© 1992 United Feature Syndicate, Inc.

BUT SOMEDAY I WANT TO HAVE CHILDREN.

LET'S HOPE THEY'RE NOT AS SELFISH AS YOU.

GEE, TIM, YOU LOOK AWFUL.

I'VE BEEN WORKING FOR FIVE DAYS WITHOUT ANY SLEEP TO FINISH THIS REPORT.

AT FIRST I HAD A MENTAL BLOCK. BUT ON THE FOURTH DAY I WAS VISITED BY AN INCAN MONKEY GOD WHO TOLD ME WHAT TO WRITE.

8-3

WOW, LUCKY BREAK.

NOW I JUST HAVE TO FIND SOMEBODY WHO CAN TRANSLATE HIS SIMPLE BUT BEAUTIFUL LANGUAGE.

© 1992 United Feature Syndicate, Inc.

I UNDERSTAND YOU'VE BEEN GOING WITHOUT SLEEP OR FOOD FOR DAYS JUST TO MEET SOME ARTIFICIAL DEADLINE.

ERGLE, FLUMG

AS A RESULT, YOUR WORK HAS BEEN MUDDLE-BRAINED AND INCOMPREHENSIBLE. YOU LEAVE ME NO CHOICE, TIM.

GLEEB, NUB

8-4

TIM GOT PROMOTED TO DIVISION MANAGER.

I WONDER IF HE KNOWS IT.

© 1992 United Feature Syndicate, Inc.

I'VE SACRIFICED MY HEALTH, MY PERSONAL LIFE AND MY SOUL TO GET PROMOTED.

HA HA HA! BUT IT WAS ALL WORTH IT BECAUSE I HAVE AN OFFICE WITH A <u>DOOR</u> AND YOU STILL WORK IN A CUBICLE!

8-5

MAYBE I'LL HOST A SPECIAL "LOW-ACHIEVER DAY" TO LET YOU TOUCH MY DOOR.

OOPS

© 1992 United Feature Syndicate, Inc.

DILBERT

By Scott Adams

WHY SHOULD I HIRE YOU AS MY CONSULTANT?

I'LL USE MY SPECIAL PROCESS OF COGNITIVE DISSONANCE TO IMPROVE EMPLOYEE MORALE.

HOW DOES IT WORK?

WHEN PEOPLE ARE IN AN ABSURD SITUATION, THEIR MINDS RATIONALIZE IT BY INVENTING A COMFORTABLE ILLUSION.

OKAY, GO DO IT.

ISN'T IT STRANGE THAT YOU HAVE THIS DEAD END JOB WHEN YOU'RE TWICE AS SMART AS YOUR BOSS?

THE HOURS ARE LONG, THE PAY IS MEDIOCRE, NOBODY RESPECTS YOUR CONTRIBUTIONS, AND YET YOU FREELY CHOOSE TO WORK HERE.

IT'S ABSURD! NO, WAIT... THERE MUST BE A REASON... I MUST WORK HERE BECAUSE I LOVE THE WORK.

I LOVE THIS JOB.

NEXT!

© 1992 United Feature Syndicate, Inc.

201

THE MIGHTY WARRIOR PREPARES FOR BATTLE...

TODAY, BOLD MEMOS WILL BE WRITTEN, DANGEROUS MEETINGS WILL BE ATTENDED, AND MANY A PHOTOCOPIED IMAGE WILL BE CAPTURED FOR ETERNITY.

IF IT WEREN'T FOR SARCASM, MY LIFE WOULD SOUND PATHETIC.

GLAD TO HELP.

I HAVEN'T DATED MUCH SINCE I CAME DOWN WITH PUPPETITIS.

IT'S A RARE DISORDER THAT MAKES YOUR HAND ACT LIKE A PUPPET.

THAT'S WEIRD.

HE HATES US! WE MUST KILL HIM!

NOT YET, GINGER!

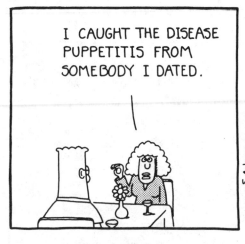

I CAUGHT THE DISEASE PUPPETITIS FROM SOMEBODY I DATED.

HA HA! THAT'S RIGHT! NOW HER HAND IS A PUPPET!

I HATE THE NINETIES.

JOIN US... DON'T BE AFRAID.

DOGBERT THE MARRIAGE COUNSELOR

WE HAVE A RUNNING FIGHT OVER HOW TO SQUEEZE THE TUBE OF TOOTHPASTE.

I LIKE TO SQUEEZE IT FROM THE BOTTOM. SHE PREFERS TO EMPTY THE TUBE ON THE RUG AND ROLL AROUND IN IT.

AT NIGHT, DOES SHE "HOG" THE BLANKETS AND SNORT?

WOW, IT'S LIKE YOU KNOW HER.

DOGBERT THE MARRIAGE COUNSELOR

I FELL IN LOVE WITH HIM BECAUSE HE HAD A GREAT CAR...

IT WASN'T UNTIL LATER THAT I REALIZED HE HAS THE PERSONALITY OF MILDEW.

HAVE YOU TRIED SPRAYING HIM WITH LYSOL?

YEAH, IT ONLY MAKES HIM DIZZY.

BILL'S BIG 'N' EGG-SHAPED MEN'S FASHIONS

SPECIALIZING IN THE OVOID MAN

OPEN

I WANT SOME CLOTHES THAT MAKE A STATEMENT.

ALL OUR CLOTHES MAKE A STATEMENT.

THIS SWEATER SAYS "HELP ME, HELP ME, I LOOK LIKE A BIG EGG!"

DOES IT COME IN BROWN?

DILBERT
By Scott Adams

I'M TAKING ORDERS FOR "CAMP GIRL COOKIES" ON BEHALF OF MY DAUGHTER.

HOW MANY DOZEN CAN I GUILT YOU INTO BUYING?

I'VE ALWAYS WONDERED, TED, WHY DO THEY SELL COOKIES? IS IT JUST FOR THE MONEY?

NO, IT'S TO HELP THEM BUILD CHARACTER BY EARNING THEIR OWN MONEY.

OH, SO YOUR DAUGHTER IS DOING SOME SELLING FROM DOOR-TO-DOOR?

NO, TOO DANGEROUS. MY WIFE AND I ARE DOING ALL THE SELLING AT WORK.

8-23

WELL, THEN AREN'T YOU ONLY TEACHING YOUR DAUGHTER TO ACT HELPLESS SO OTHER PEOPLE WILL DO HER WORK?

JUST BUY THE STUPID COOKIES!!

HAVE YOU CONSIDERED FOSTER CARE FOR YOUR KIDS?

THERE ARE TWO GOOD ARTICLES IN THE PAPER TODAY; ONE ABOUT MAGNETS, AND ONE ON SIGN LANGUAGE.

I'D LIKE YOU TO WRITE A WHITE PAPER ON HOW THESE ITEMS COULD INFLUENCE THE PROJECT YOU'RE WORKING ON.

DO YOU EVEN KNOW WHAT PROJECT I'M WORKING ON?

I DON'T HAVE TIME TO GET INTO MINUTIA.

LET'S BEGIN BY GOING AROUND THE TABLE AND INTRODUCING OURSELVES.

I'M DILBERT. I'VE WORKED FOR YOU FOR FIVE YEARS.

ALBERT, SIX YEARS.

ALICE, I'VE WORKED FOR YOU FOR TEN YEARS.

SALLY, EIGHT YEARS.

I KNEW THESE PEOPLE LOOKED FAMILIAR.

THANK YOU ALL FOR COMING. THERE'S NO SPECIFIC AGENDA FOR THIS MEETING...

AS USUAL, WE'LL JUST MAKE UNRELATED EMOTIONAL STATEMENTS ABOUT THINGS WHICH BOTHER US. I'LL KICK IT OFF...

THERE'S NEVER TIME TO GET ANY WORK DONE AROUND HERE!!

DILBERT

By Scott Adams

THE PROBLEM WITH MODERN SOCIETY IS THAT WE HAVE NO TRADITIONS.

WE SHOULD CREATE SOME TRADITIONS FOR FUTURE GENERATIONS.

HOW DO YOU CREATE A TRADITION?

WELL, YOU JUST DO SOMETHING RIDICULOUS EVERY YEAR AT THE SAME TIME.

EVENTUALLY OTHER PEOPLE JOIN IN AND THEN IT'S A TRADITION.

OOH, HOW ABOUT "ANNUAL NOSE-SAUSAGE DAY"? YOU DRESS IN COLORFUL ROBES AND STICK SAUSAGES IN YOUR NOSE!

YES, YES... AND WE'LL DO A SQUIRREL DANCE AND SHOUT "KALOO KALAH" AT THE SUN!

OR MAYBE NOT.

YOU LOST ME WITH THE SQUIRREL DANCE.

I'M SENDING ALL OF YOU TO THE "RIVERS AND TREES" MANAGEMENT COURSE.

THERE YOU'LL BE ASKED TO PERFORM A VARIETY OF DANGEROUS TASKS IN THE WOODS. YOUR SURVIVAL WILL DEPEND ON YOUR CREATIVITY AND ABILITY TO WORK TOGETHER.

8-31

OH, SO IT'S A TEAM-BUILDING EXERCISE.

I THINK OF IT MORE AS A HEADCOUNT REDUCTION THING.

AT THE "RIVERS AND TREES" MANAGEMENT COURSE.

WE'LL START WITH A TRUST-BUILDING EXERCISE.

YOU HAVE ONE MINUTE TO DECIDE TO EAT THESE DONUTS OR TO SAVE YOUR CO-WORKER FROM THE BEAR.

OKAY, WHO WANTS TO BE ON THE DONUT OPTION WORKING COMMITTEE?

OOPS... PROBLEM SOLVED.

9-1

AT THE "RIVERS AND TREES" MANAGEMENT COURSE.

NEXT, WE HAVE A CREATIVITY EXERCISE.

YOUR TASK IS TO BUILD A COMMERCIAL AIRPORT LANDING STRIP USING NOTHING BUT A LEAF AND A DEAD BEE.

9-2

LOOK, WE ALREADY VOTED. WE'RE DESIGN AND YOU'RE CONSTRUCTION.

TIME.

AT THE "RIVERS AND TREES" MANAGEMENT COURSE.

THIS NEXT EXERCISE IS ALWAYS A FAVORITE.

USING ONLY A ROPE, YOUR TEAM MUST FIGURE OUT HOW TO CROSS THE MUDDY PATCH WITHOUT GETTING YOUR FEET DIRTY.

9-3

I COULD HAVE BEEN A FOREST RANGER, BUT NO-O-O-O...

I'M CHANNELING ALL OF MY PAIN AND HOSTILITY INTO MY ART.

9-4

ALL I SEE IS A BOWL OF FRUIT.

THE BANANA HATES THE APPLE.

TELL ME WHAT YOU THINK, AND DON'T TRY TO SPARE MY FEELINGS.

IT'S A HIDEOUS COMPOST OF RANDOM COLORS. IT SEEMS BOTH HACKNEYED AND POORLY EXECUTED. IT'S AN EMBARRASSING PROOF OF YOUR UTTER LACK OF TALENT.

9-5

AS FOR YOU PERSONALLY, SPEND SOME TIME ON A "STAIRMASTER."

STICK TO THE ART, PLEASE!

IT'S CALLED MULTIMEDIA, DOGBERT. NOW I CAN INCLUDE VIDEO AND MUSIC WITH MY COMPUTER PROGRAMS.

THIS MORNING I ADDED MY FACE PLUS THE THEME SONG FROM "STAR WARS" TO MY BUDGET SPREADSHEET.

9-7

I ALREADY FORGOT HOW I SURVIVED WITHOUT IT.

IT CAN GET PRETTY UGLY WHEN SCIENCE AND ART COLLIDE.

WHEN I STARTED PROGRAMMING, WE DIDN'T HAVE ANY OF THESE SISSY "ICONS" AND "WINDOWS."

ALL WE HAD WERE ZEROS AND ONES -- AND SOMETIMES WE DIDN'T EVEN HAVE ONES.

9-8

I WROTE AN ENTIRE DATABASE PROGRAM USING ONLY ZEROS.

YOU HAD ZEROS? WE HAD TO USE THE LETTER "O."

I'M TESTING MY THEORY THAT GOOD ADVERTISING CAN SELL ANYTHING.

SO I ASKED MYSELF "WHAT IS THE THING LEAST DESIRED ON EARTH?"

9-9

LADIES! DATE A DILBERT CALL 510-803-9338

QUANTITIES ARE LIMITED

HMM...

DILBERT

By Scott Adams

HI, RATBERT. MAY I HAVE SOME CHIPS?

NO, SORRY. THERE ARE ONLY ENOUGH FOR ONE.

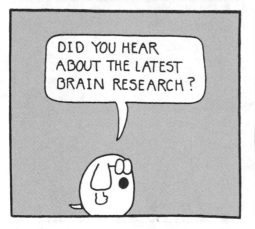

DID YOU HEAR ABOUT THE LATEST BRAIN RESEARCH?

SCIENCE HAS PROVEN THAT THE PART OF THE BRAIN RESPONSIBLE FOR CONSCIOUS THOUGHT DOESN'T SHOW ANY STIMULATION UNTIL AFTER YOU ACT.

THAT MEANS YOU NEVER MAKE CONSCIOUS DECISIONS; ALL YOU DO IS RATIONALIZE WHAT YOU'VE DONE AFTER THE FACT.

YOUR LIFE IS NOTHING BUT A SERIES OF ABSURD RATIONALIZATIONS FOR THE RANDOM INTERACTION OF CHEMICALS IN YOUR BRAIN.

BLINK BLINK

AAAGH!!! MY LIFE IS ABSURD!!

THAT WAS MEAN, BUT ARGUABLY I COULDN'T CONTROL MYSELF.

© 1992 United Feature Syndicate, Inc.

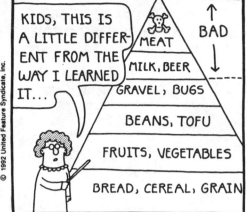

DILBERT By Scott Adams

HA HA! NOW SPIN ON YOUR HEAD! HA HA HA!

WHAT'S GOING ON HERE?

THIS IS YERGI. HE'S VISITING FROM ELBONIA.

THE ECONOMY IN ELBONIA IS SO BAD HE ONLY EARNS THREE DOLLARS A MONTH AS A DOCTOR.

IT TAKES A YEAR TO EARN ENOUGH FOR A PAIR OF SHOES... IT TAKES TWO YEARS FOR A POUND OF MEAT.

PHILANTHROPIST THAT I AM, I OFFERED TO GIVE HIM AN OLD BOOT IF HE WOULD ACT LIKE MY TRAINED MONKEY FOR A WEEK.

DOGBERT! I CAN'T BELIEVE YOU WOULD BUY THIS MAN'S DIGNITY FOR AN OLD BOOT!

9-20

I PLAN TO TELL THE KIDS IT'S A POUND OF MEAT.

QUIET, BOBO.

THERE... I THINK I'VE INVENTED A WAY TO SEND VAST AMOUNTS OF DATA WITHOUT FIBER OPTIC CABLES.

IT'S A SIMPLE APPLICATION OF J.S. BELL'S THEOREM.* HE SHOWED THAT IF YOU BREAK UP A MOLECULE AND CHANGE THE SPIN OF ONE ELECTRON, THE SPIN OF THE OTHER ELECTRONS ORIGINALLY JOINED WILL IMMEDIATELY CHANGE TOO, NO MATTER WHERE THEY ARE.

* Really, no kidding

WHAT DO YOU THINK THE FIBER OPTIC INDUSTRY WILL GIVE ME FOR THIS?

A HORSE'S HEAD IN YOUR BED.

FROM THE LOOKS OF YOUR GARBAGE, YOU'VE INVENTED SOME SORT OF MOLECULE BIFURCATION COMMUNICATOR.

AH, YES, EINSTEIN THOUGHT THIS TYPE OF THING MIGHT WORK. PHYSICIST JOHN STUART BELL KIND OF FLESHED IT OUT IN 1964. BUT YOU'VE REALLY ADDED SOMETHING...

SPECIFICALLY, YOU'VE ADDED THIS CALCULATION ERROR HERE.

HIS NAME IS DILBERT. HE INVENTED SOMETHING THAT WOULD MAKE OUR ENTIRE PRODUCT LINE OBSOLETE.

DO YOU HAVE A PLAN?

UH... I COULD WAX YOUR DESK WITH MY HAIR AGAIN.

IT'S JUST CRAZY ENOUGH TO WORK.

I'VE RECEIVED DEATH THREATS BECAUSE OF MY NEW PATENT. SO I AUGMENTED OUR HOME SECURITY SYSTEM.

THE SIDEWALK IS RIGGED TO GIVE AN ELECTRIC SHOCK, THUS DISARMING THE INTRUDER. THEN A SPRING CATAPULTS HIM TO THE CITY LANDFILL.

AAGH! FLING

THE MAIL IS HERE.

I HEARD YOU'RE LOOKING FOR A HIT MAN TO ELIMINATE AN INVENTOR NAMED DILBERT.

FOR A MILLION DOLLARS I CAN DELIVER HIS HEAD ON A PLATTER.

DOES IT HAVE TO BE ON A PLATTER? I'VE TRIED USING THOSE TUPPERWARE LETTUCE CRISPERS, BUT IT LOSES A LOT OF THE DRAMA.

HERE IS PHOTO PROOF THAT I COMPLETED MY HIT-MAN CONTRACT ON DILBERT.

EXCELLENT.

HERE HE IS, SITTING LIFELESS IN HIS STUFFED CHAIR.

IT LOOKS LIKE HE'S JUST WATCHING TELEVISION. TECHNICALLY, MY CONTRACT DOESN'T SAY I MUST KILL HIM. IT SAYS I MUST "PROVE HE HAS NO LIFE."

I'VE DECIDED TO BECOME A DEMAGOGUE.

I'LL FIND SOME ISSUE THAT APPEALS TO THE EMOTIONS AND BLIND PREJUDICES OF THE MASSES, THEN I'LL WHIP IT INTO A MEDIA FRENZY AND BECOME A NATIONAL FIGURE.

FOR EXAMPLE, UNMARRIED MEN ARE RESPONSIBLE FOR MOST OF OF OUR VIOLENT CRIMES.

THAT'S BECAUSE WE TEND TO HAVE PETS.

9-28

"UNMARRIED MEN COMMIT NINETY PERCENT OF ALL VIOLENT ACTS. THEY SHOULD ALL BE JAILED IN ADVANCE TO PREVENT FURTHER ATROCITIES."

"AND I SHOULD BECOME A MEDIA SENSATION FOR SUGGESTING SUCH A PROVOCATIVE THING.

THE END "

IT'S HARD TO WRITE A WHOLE BOOK WHEN YOU'RE AS GIFTED AS I AM AT GETTING TO THE POINT.

9-29

MY GUEST FOR TODAY'S SHOW IS DOGBERT, AUTHOR OF THE ONE-PAGE BOOK "UNMARRIED MEN ARE SCUM."

YOUR THEORY IS THAT ALL UNMARRIED MEN SHOULD BE JAILED FOR LIFE, THUS ENDING MOST CRIME.

EXACTLY.

9-30

WHAT IF THEY TRY TO BEAT THE SYSTEM BY GETTING MARRIED?

SERVES 'EM RIGHT.

I'M FOLLOWING IN YOUR FOOTSTEPS SO I CAN BE A DEMAGOGUE TOO.

YOUR BOOK "UNMARRIED MEN ARE SCUM" WAS SO SUCCESSFUL THAT I DECIDED TO WRITE MY OWN HATE BOOK DISGUISED AS SCIENCE!

10-1

I CALL IT "MOLES ARE MORONS."

WERE YOU AWARE THAT MOLES HAVE A STRONG UNDER- GROUND MOVE- MENT?

I MUST WARN YOU THAT I HAVE AN OBSESSIVE PERSON- ALITY.

IF I SPEND A MOMENT WITH A MAN I FALL COMPLETELY IN LOVE. I THINK OF ONLY HIM. I...I BECOME HIS SLAVE.

10-2

ARE YOU SAYING...

YES. I'M IN LOVE WITH OUR WAITER.

HAVE YOU EVER HAD A STRANGE DREAM OR A NOSEBLEED?

YES.

IT'S CLEAR THAT YOU'RE SUPPRESSING MEMORIES OF BEING ABDUCTED BY ALIENS. I CAN USE HYPNOSIS TO GET AT THOSE MEMORIES.

10-3

WHAT IF THE HYPNOSIS ITSELF MAKES ME THINK IT HAPPENED WHEN IT DIDN'T? I'LL BE SCORNED AND RIDICULED FOR LIFE.

THAT'S A RISK I'M WILLING TO TAKE.

DILBERT

By Scott Adams

DO YOU THINK IT'S BETTER TO BE SMART OR GOOD-LOOKING, DOGBERT.

I'VE BEEN BOTH FOR SO LONG, IT'S HARD TO BE OBJECTIVE.

IT'S HYPOTHETICAL. SUPPOSE YOU HAD TO PICK ONE.

I'D STAY AS I AM: SMART, GOOD-LOOKING AND TALENTED.

YOU CAN'T ADD STUFF. YOU HAVE TO START WITH NOTHING AND PICK EITHER BRAINS OR GOOD LOOKS.

AND WITTY TOO... SMART, GOOD-LOOKING, TALENTED AND WITTY.

NO, NO, NO... SUPPOSE YOU HAD <u>NONE</u> OF THOSE QUALITIES. WHAT WOULD YOU DO THEN?

10-4

I'D PROBABLY ANNOY MY DOG. SAME AS YOU.

THE GOVERNMENT SENT A GENERAL TO KILL ME FOR TALKING ABOUT MY ENCOUNTER WITH SPACE ALIENS.

I WAS SCARED AT FIRST. BUT WHEN YOU THINK ABOUT THE GOVERNMENT'S TRACK RECORD, WELL, MY ODDS ARE PRETTY GOOD...

ESPECIALLY AFTER ALL THE BUDGET CUTBACKS.

DANG IT! WHERE'S MY AIR SUPPORT?!!

GENERAL, I DON'T UNDERSTAND WHY THE GOVERNMENT IS TRYING TO COVER UP ALL THE U.F.O. ENCOUNTERS.

PEOPLE WOULD LOSE FAITH IN THEIR GOVERNMENT IF THEY KNEW ALIENS WERE ABDUCTING PEOPLE AND WE WERE HELPLESS TO STOP THEM.

SO, TO MAINTAIN CONFIDENCE IN THE GOVERNMENT, YOU USE OUR TAXES TO KILL THE CITIZENS WHO FIND OUT?

IS THAT SO BAD?

WE CAN ONLY SPECULATE WHY ALIENS KEEP ABDUCTING PEOPLE.

THEY OFTEN PROBE PEOPLE'S BODY CAVITIES. SOMETIMES THEY IMPLANT SMALL OBJECTS. IT MUST BE SOME FORM OF HIGHLY ADVANCED MEDICAL RESEARCH.

HOW ABOUT ANOTHER ROUND OF "HIDE THE PELLET"?

OKAY. I CAN USE MY NOSE PROBER.

DILBERT
By Scott Adams

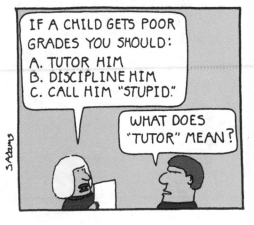

WE'D BETTER CHECK IT OUT.

PARENT LICENSES

WHY DO WE NEED A LICENSE TO BECOME PARENTS?

SOMETHING HAD TO BE DONE.

UNDER THE OLD SYSTEM ALL YOU NEEDED TO BE A PARENT WAS A FEW BODY PARTS AND A BRAIN THE SIZE OF A GARBANZO BEAN.

SO I DEVELOPED THIS WRITTEN TEST TO WEED OUT THE MAJOR BOZOS.

IF A BABY CRIES, YOU SHOULD:
A. FEED IT
B. DISCIPLINE IT
C. CALL IT "STUPID"

YOU HAVE TO SHOW IT WHO'S THE BOSS.

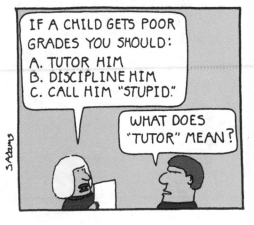

IF A CHILD GETS POOR GRADES YOU SHOULD:
A. TUTOR HIM
B. DISCIPLINE HIM
C. CALL HIM "STUPID."

WHAT DOES "TUTOR" MEAN?

AN ACCEPTABLE NICKNAME FOR A CHILD IS:
A. JUNIOR
B. UGLY
C. STUPID

DEPENDS IF IT'S A BOY.

10-11

WELL? CAN WE BE PARENTS?

NO. AND YOU'LL HAVE TO LEAVE SOME BODY PARTS AT THE FRONT DESK.

S.Adams

I JUST RECEIVED YOUR EMPLOYEE SUGGESTION.

WE'LL HANDLE IT THE USUAL WAY -- BY MAKING YOU SIT UNDER A WET BLANKET SURROUNDED BY IMBECILES.

10-15

AT LEAST THERE'S A PROCESS.

EXPLAIN YOUR SUGGESTION AGAIN.

MOST HANDSOME MEN ARE SELF-CENTERED JERKS.

BUT YOU'RE DIFFERENT... YOU'RE ...

10-16

CONSIDERATE?

UGLY.

REMEMBER THE TIME YOU LAUGHED AT YOUR OWN JOKE SO HARD THAT YOU INHALED AND SNORTED AT THE SAME TIME?

THEN YOU CHOKED ON YOUR OWN SPIT, WHICH CAUSED YOU TO LURCH OVER AND BONK YOUR HEAD ON THE COFFEE TABLE...

I'M IGNORING YOU.

WHO SAYS YOUR LIFE IS BORING?

10-17

I'VE DECIDED TO BECOME A DOCTOR.

PEOPLE HAVE TO SUCK UP TO DOCTORS, OTHERWISE THEY STICK BIG NEEDLES INTO YOUR BODY FOR PRACTICALLY NO REASON AT ALL.

A LOT OF CAREERS DON'T OFFER THAT KIND OPPORTUNITY.

YEAH, IT'S NOT THE SAME WITH A STAPLER.

10-19

HOLD STILL WHILE DOCTOR DOGBERT WHACKS YOUR KNEE.

10-20

AAK... CRIME IS SOCIETY'S FAULT... RAISE TAXES TO FEED THE POOR... STOP NUCLEAR RESEARCH... SAVE THE...

TAP

APPARENTLY YOU'RE A KNEE-JERK LIBERAL. YOU CAN LIVE A NORMAL LIFE BUT YOU'LL BE ANNOYING AT PARTIES.

YOU HAVE A MILD FLU, AND NORMALLY YOU WOULD SURVIVE.

HOWEVER, IN THIS BRIEF VISIT I'VE DEVELOPED NO REAL EMPATHY FOR YOU, SO I'VE DECIDED TO LET YOU DIE.

IS THERE ANYTHING I CAN DO?!

WELL... UNLESS YOU CAN AFFORD MY NEW "AMBASSADOR CLASS" SERVICE.

10-21

DILBERT

By Scott Adams

DILBERT, I THINK IT WOULD BE BETTER IF WE WERE JUST FRIENDS.

OKAY.

OKAY?? HE TOOK IT TOO EASY. I SHOULD BARGAIN FOR MORE.

I MEAN... FRIENDS WITH OTHER PEOPLE. YOU AND I WOULD JUST BE ACQUAINTANCES.

OKAY.

STILL TOO EASY. I CAN GET MORE.

I DON'T MEAN THE KIND OF ACQUAINTANCES THAT COULD BECOME FRIENDS... IT WOULD BE MORE LIKE YOU WERE AN EX-EMPLOYEE OF MINE.

OKAY.

YEAH, THAT'S IT. YOU CAN BE MY EX-BUTLER, WHO I FIRED FOR STEALING STUFF.

OKAY.

10-25

WHAT'S GOING ON HERE?

GOOD. IT LOOKS LIKE THE WINDOW OF OPPORTUNITY IS STILL SLIGHTLY OPEN.

SO, YOU'RE A TIME MANAGEMENT EXPERT HUH? MIGHT BE USEFUL... I'LL LET YOU KNOW...

DECIDE NOW! DO IT! DO IT, DO IT! NOW NOW NOW NOW!

10-26

YOU'RE GOOD... WHEN CAN YOU START?

I'LL GET BACK TO YOU.

S. Adams

WELCOME TO THE "DOGBERT TIME MANAGEMENT LECTURE SERIES."

SORRY I'M AN HOUR LATE, BUT I WAS GIVING ANOTHER LECTURE ACROSS TOWN... IN EFFECT, I'LL COMPLETE TWO JOBS WHILE YOU SIT IN THE DARK LIKE STUNNED CATTLE.

I DON'T MEAN TO RUB IT IN, BUT MOOOO...

10-27

EVERY PERSON HAS NATURAL DAILY RHYTHMS OF MENTAL PEAKS AND TROUGHS. WE CAN USE THIS KNOWLEDGE TO IMPROVE YOUR PERFORMANCE.

10-28

WE USE HOURLY BODY TEMPERATURE READINGS TO IDENTIFY AND AVOID THE TROUGHS.

One o'clock. We have encountered a severe trough. I fear it could be the dreaded "El Niño" trough.

S. Adams

235

I'M AFRAID YOUR COMPANY IS BEING HIT BY AN EL NIÑO CIRCADIAN TROUGH.

WHAT'S THAT?

ONCE A DECADE, THE NATURAL BODY RHYTHMS OF ALL THE EMPLOYEES REACH THEIR MENTAL LOW POINT AT THE SAME TIME.

IT'S BEST TO AVOID ANY FORM OF MENTAL ACTIVITY.

STAFF MEETING!

LET ME SHOW YOU WHERE THE INFORMATION IS IN YOUR BINDER.

FIRST, I'LL NEED A GOOD LOAD OF SALIVA ON MY PAGE-TURNING HAND.

SLURP SLURP

MAYBE YOU CAN SHOW ME IN YOUR BINDER.

CAN'T... SOMEHOW MY PAGES GOT ALL STUCK TOGETHER.

IT'S AMAZING THAT PEOPLE BELIEVE IN ASTROLOGY... AS IF THE STARS COULD AFFECT YOUR PERSONALITY.

WELL, SEASONAL DIFFERENCES IN DIET, SUNLIGHT AND NATURAL RHYTHMS COULD AFFECT EXPECTANT MOTHERS, WHICH COULD HAVE PREDICTABLE RESULTS ON FETAL BRAIN DEVELOPMENT.

MAYBE THE ANCIENTS SIMPLY USED THE STARS TO MEASURE THE TIMING OF THESE PATTERNS.

IF THEY WERE SO SMART, WHY DIDN'T THEY INVENT WATCHES?

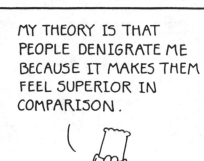

WHAT HAPPENED TO YOU?

I ASKED FLOYD A QUESTION.

FLOYD HATES HIS JOB, SO HE TAKES IT OUT ON CO-WORKERS. HE ALMOST CHEWED MY CLOTHES OFF.

HOW'D YOU STOP HIM?

HE WENT INTO SYNTHETIC SHOCK; IT'S NOT HEALTHY TO EAT TOO MUCH OF THIS STUFF.

WHAT?! YOU THINK I'LL HELP YOU JUST BECAUSE I'M YOUR CO-WORKER?? HA! I HATE CO-WORKERS!

ALL I NEED IS...

I HATE THIS JOB! I HATE EVERYTHING! THE ONLY THING I LIKE IS BEING MEAN TO CO-WORKERS WHO NEED THE VITAL INFORMATION THAT I CONTROL!

IF YOU THINK YOU HATE HIM, YOU SHOULD TRY BEING HIS SECRETARY.

EVERYBODY PICK A STRAW. THE LOSER HAS TO KILL OUR ABUSIVE CO-WORK-ER, FLOYD.

DILBERT LOSES. HE PICKED THE BLUE STRAW.

I THOUGHT THE SHORT STRAW LOSES.

YOU'RE ALREADY A MURDERER; DON'T BE A CHEAT-ER TOO.

DILBERT By Scott Adams

THE TINY NATION OF ELBONIA HAS ERUPTED IN CIVIL WAR.

WHAT CAUSED YOU TO TURN YOUR WEAPONS ON YOUR OWN PEOPLE?

WEAPONS? WE CAN USE WEAPONS?

WELL, NO WONDER IT WAS TAKING SO LONG.

11-16

THE PRESIDENT OF ELBONIA ASKED ME TO NEGOTIATE AN END TO THEIR CIVIL WAR.

WHY YOU?

NO DOUBT HE WAS IMPRESSED BY MY DIPLOMACY WHEN I WAS AN ECONOMIC ADVISOR... I JUST WISH I DIDN'T HAVE TO FLY ON ELBONIA AIRLINES.

11-17

ELBONIA

...AT HIS WEIGHT, WE CALCULATE THAT ELBONIA AIRLINES WILL FLING HIM RIGHT ON THE REBEL LEADER.

DILBERT TAKES ELBONIA AIRLINES. HE'S BEEN ASKED TO NEGOTIATE AN END TO THE ELBONIAN CIVIL WAR.

I CAN SUCCEED IF I FIND SOME WAY TO IMPRESS THE REBEL LEADER THEY CALL "THE FOX."

THE FOX IS DEAD!!

11-18

11-22

© 1992 United Feature Syndicate, Inc.

WE LEFT-HANDED ELBONIANS HAVE BEEN PERSECUTED FOR CENTURIES. WE MUST CRUSH THE RIGHTIES!

DON'T YOU SEE THAT IT'S ONLY AN ARBITRARY DISTINCTION? ISN'T IT OBVIOUS THAT PEOPLE ARE THE SAME NO MATTER WHAT HAND THEY FAVOR?

NO, THAT ISN'T OBVIOUS TO US AT ALL.

GEEZ, YOU LEFTIES ARE THICK. I'M GLAD I'M NORMAL.

ELBONIANS HEAR ME! YOU MUST END YOUR FUTILE CIVIL WAR.

YOU'VE BEEN LOVING YOUR ANIMALS AND FIGHTING EACH OTHER. A CIVILIZED COUNTRY SHOULD SLAUGHTER THE ANIMALS AND SIMPLY DISCRIMINATE ECONOMICALLY AGAINST EACH OTHER!

HOW DID MY SPEECH GO OVER?

I'M SOLD, BUT I THINK THE SECRETARY OF STATE WAS A BIT PUT OFF.

I ALWAYS THOUGHT YOU BEAVERS WERE BUSY ALL THE TIME.

THAT'S A COMMON STEREOTYPE. I'M ACTUALLY QUITE LAZY.

HOW DO YOU BUILD YOUR BEAVER HOME?

I RENT.

WHEN YOU'RE A LAZY BEAVER, YOU TRY TO FIND SHORTCUTS AND TRICKS TO GET YOUR WORK DONE.

I GOT THIS DAYTIME PLANNER TO ORGANIZE MY DAY MORE EFFICIENTLY.

BUT ALL IT DOES IS SIT THERE.

LOOKS LIKE YOU GOT A BAD ONE.

JUST TAKE ONE, RATBERT.

AAARGH!! I'M CHANGING! I'M CHANGING!

IT WASN'T FUNNY THE FIRST HUNDRED TIMES I GAVE YOU A TIC-TAC EITHER.

LET'S TRY IT AGAIN!

THE ROOF IS LEAKING THERE. CAN YOU FIX IT TOMORROW?

WELL, LIKE ALL MEMBERS OF MY PROFESSION, I'M UNRELIABLE. HOWEVER, I COULD GIVE YOU A QUOTE AND THEN NEVER SHOW UP OR RETURN YOUR CALLS.

YOU'RE HIRED. NOBODY ELSE WOULD EVEN SHOW UP FOR THE QUOTE.

I DEPEND ON REPEAT CUSTOMERS.

DILBERT

By Scott Adams

I DISCOVERED A NEW TOOL FOR MEETING WOMEN.

A METAL DETECTOR?

EXACTLY. I'LL BE NONCHALANTLY USING IT IN THE PARK...

AND YOU'LL FIND BURIED WOMEN WHO HAVE METAL PLATES IN THEIR HEADS?

DON'T BE RIDICULOUS. THE ODDS OF FINDING A LIVE ONE ARE ABOUT A JILLION TO ONE.

NO, I PLAN TO APPEAL TO WOMEN'S NATURAL SCIENTIFIC CURIOSITY.

THEY'LL STRIKE UP CONVERSATIONS ABOUT HOW THE METAL DETECTOR WORKS ... AND WHERE THEY CAN BUY ONE.

11-29

OOH, I'D BETTER BRING A NOTE PAD TO WRITE DOWN ALL THE PHONE NUMBERS.

ON ONE PAW, I WANT TO HELP HIM. ON THE OTHER PAW, MAYBE IT'S BETTER IF HE DOESN'T EVER REPRODUCE.

WHAT DO YOU THINK OF MY DISGUISE?

I'M GOING TO TELL THE MEDIA THAT I'M A SPACE ALIEN WITH UNSTOPPABLE POWERS. WITH LUCK, THE NATIONS OF THE WORLD WILL SURRENDER WITHOUT A FIGHT.

11-30

YOU THINK PEOPLE ARE IDIOTS... DON'T YOU?

THIS IS WHAT I LOOKED LIKE BEFORE THE DISGUISE.

AS MY ANTENNAE CLEARLY PROVE, I'M A SPACE ALIEN WITH INCREDIBLE POWERS.

I CALL ON THE NATIONS OF THE WORLD TO SURRENDER. OTHERWISE, I WILL CAUSE YOUR STOCK MARKETS TO FALL.

LATER

THE MARKET FELL FIVE POINTS TODAY. ANALYSTS BLAME INTEREST RATES AND ALIENS.

YES!

THE LEADERS OF THE WORLD MET TODAY TO CONSIDER THE DEMANDS OF DOGBERT THE SPACE ALIEN.

ALL IN FAVOR OF LETTING THE ALIEN RUN THE WORLD, RAISE YOUR HAND.

U.N.

MEANWHILE IN THE TRANSLATORS' BOOTH, A RECKLESS PRANK IS BEING PLAYED.

HE SAYS "WHO WANTS MY PARKING SPACE BY THE ELEVATOR?"

12-2

IN A SURPRISE DECISION, THE UNITED NATIONS VOTED TO MAKE DOGBERT—THE SPACE ALIEN—THE SUPREME RULER OF EARTH.

MORE ON THAT LATER. BUT FIRST, SCIENCE OFFERS NEW HOPE FOR PEOPLE WITH FRECKLES...

DOGBERT HOLDS HIS FIRST PRESS CONFERENCE

HU-HA-HA! HU-HA-HA!

NOT A GOOD SIGN.

NOW THAT YOU'RE THE SUPREME RULER OF EARTH, WILL YOU BECOME MORALLY CORRUPT?

YES, THAT'S MY PLAN. IT'S REALLY THE ONLY WAY TO ENJOY A JOB LIKE THIS.

AND OF COURSE I'LL BE RAISING TAXES JUST TO SEE THE EXPRESSIONS ON YOUR FACES.

STOP! I AM THE "AMAZING RONNY,", FAMOUS SKEPTIC AND DEBUNKER.

I WILL PROVE TO THE MEDIA THAT YOU'RE NOT A POWERFUL SPACE ALIEN AT ALL.

SEE HOW EASILY THE MEDIA WERE DUPED?

THERE'S STILL TIME TO INTERVIEW THE COW WHO DOES ALGEBRA.

RRRR

DILBERT

By Scott Adams

DOGBERT'S HOME SAFETY TIPS

IT COULD SAVE YOUR LIFE!

TIP #1: CHILDREN CAN SWALLOW ANYTHING SMALLER THAN A SOFA. ATTACH BOARDS TO VULNERABLE APPLIANCES.

HA HA! NICE TRY, BILLY!

MMPH!

TIP #2: YOUR HOUSEHOLD MAY HAVE A MEMBER WHO CAN LEGALLY VOTE BUT PROBABLY SHOULDN'T.

TRY TRICKING THEM INTO MISSING THE ELECTION.

WE'RE A COMMUNIST REGIME NOW. YOU DON'T HAVE TO VOTE.

SHOOT!

TIP #3: YOUR TELEVISION IS TRYING TO STEAL YOUR LIFE'S SAVINGS.

I PERSONALLY PRAY OVER EVERY CHECK YOU SEND.

YOUR ONLY HOPE IS TO PUSH YOUR TELEVISION OUT A HIGH WINDOW.

12-6

IF EVERYBODY DOES IT, WE JUST MIGHT GET LUCKY.

S. Adams

WHAT'S THE STORY WITH THE COSTUME, WALLY?

THE BOSS PUT ME ON A SPECIAL TASK FORCE TO SEE IF HUMOR INCREASES CREATIVITY. I HAVE TO DRESS LIKE THIS FOR A MONTH.

12-10

ARE YOU FEELING MORE CREATIVE?

YEAH. I'VE ALREADY THOUGHT OF SIX HUNDRED WAYS TO KILL HIM.

AS PART OF MY PROGRAM TO USE MORE HUMOR AT WORK, I'M ASKING EACH OF YOU TO WEAR A "KICK ME" SIGN.

12-11

I'LL CHECK LATER TO SEE IF YOU'RE MORE RELAXED AND CREATIVE.

LATER...

YOU SEEM TO BE TAKING UNFAIR ADVANTAGE OF THE SITUATION, ALICE.

OUR VIDEO GAME DIVISION HAS REACHED A SALES PLATEAU.

KIDS ARE SPENDING MORE TIME OUTSIDE THESE DAYS. THERE'S ONLY ONE THING WE CAN DO.

12-12

DIVERSIFY?

POLLUTE!

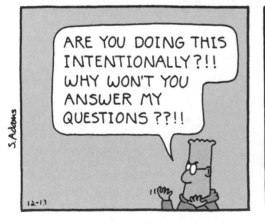